MAX COLE

MAX COLE

ENDLESS JOURNEY

RADIUS BOOKS

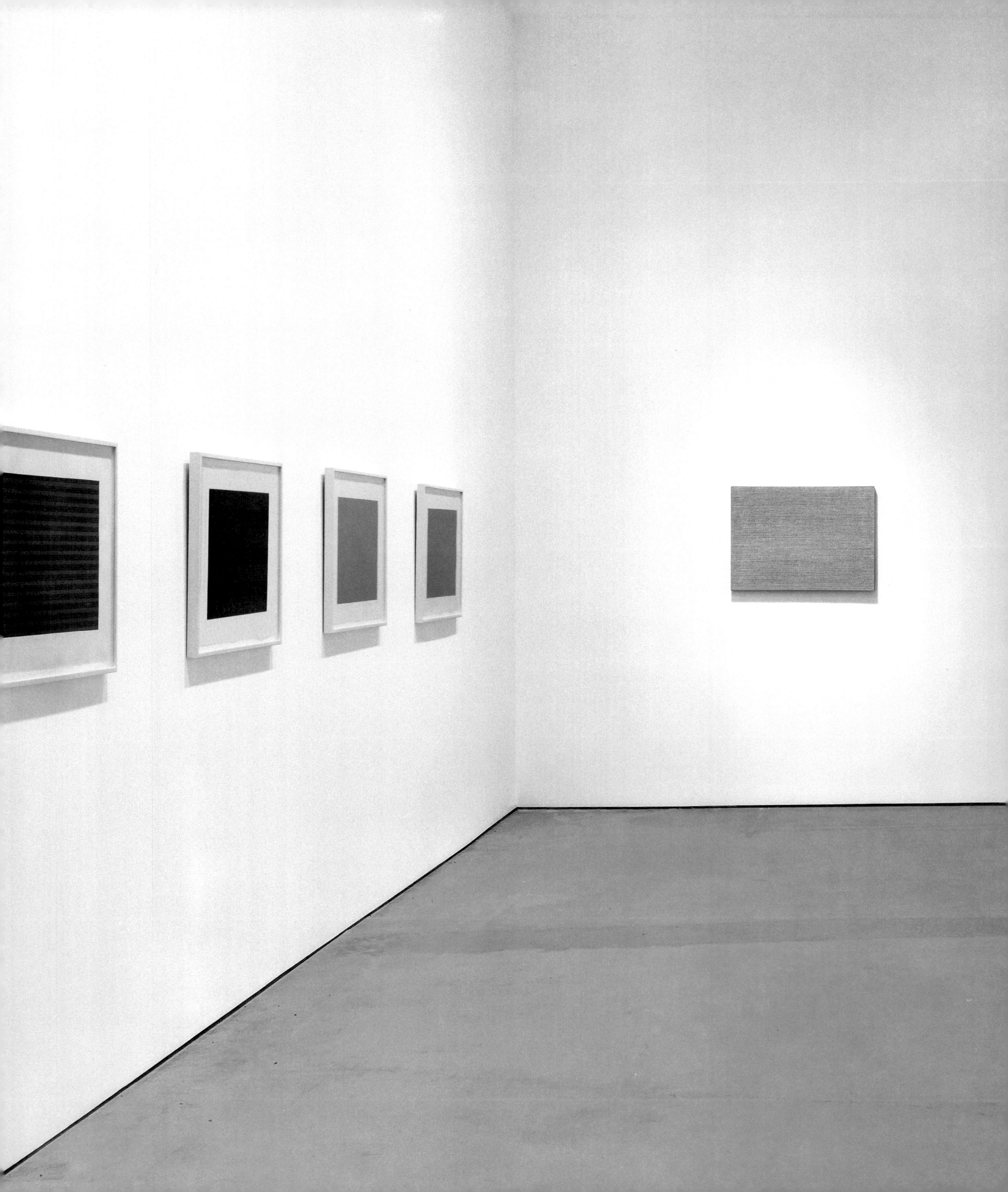

CONTENTS

09 Introduction
— LOUIS GRACHOS

13 Plates

99 Conversation with Max Cole
— DAVID PAGEL

109 Acknowledgments

111 Contributors

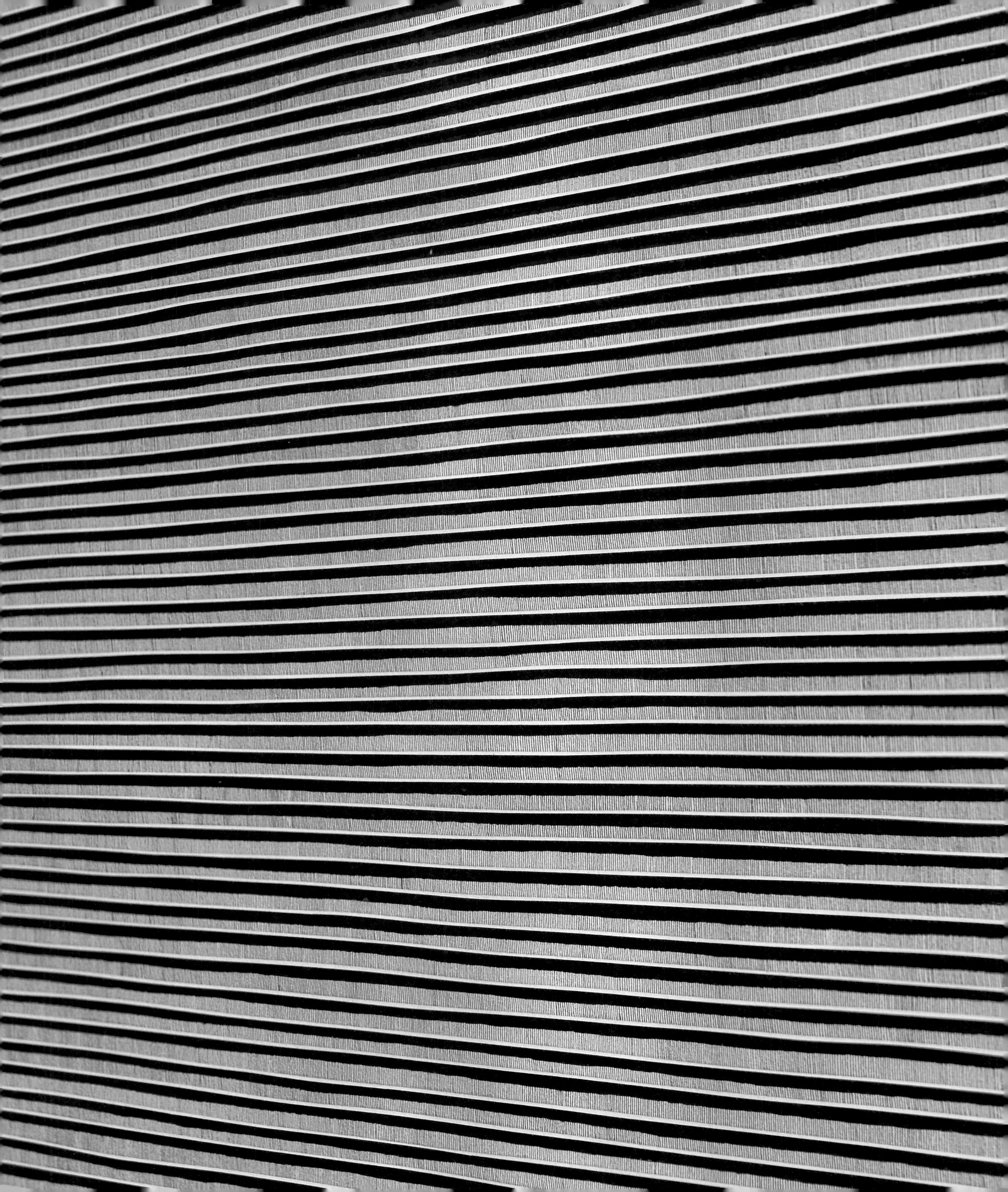

INTRODUCTION

—LOUIS GRACHOS

Phillips Executive Director, SITE Santa Fe

I was first introduced to Max Cole's work in the early 2000s when I went to visit Giuseppe Panza and view the Panza Collection in Varese, Italy. I was immediately transfixed by the beautiful, meditative, and calming quality of the paintings. I was compelled to spend a great deal of time with the works, mesmerized by the brilliance of her mark-making and her ability to create veritable poetry on the canvas. This first experience with Max's work stuck with me, and a few years later, I had the opportunity to work with Max and present several of her paintings at the Albright Knox Art Gallery in Buffalo, New York. I also had the great pleasure of securing a number of Max's paintings from the Panza Collection for the Albright Knox's collection.

When I learned that Max Cole had moved to Las Vegas, New Mexico, I seized the opportunity to present a large-scale exhibition of her work at SITE Santa Fe and to give audiences an overview of Max's extraordinary six-decade career. It was an absolute joy to work with Max on her exhibition, *Endless Journey*. SITE Santa Fe Curator Brandee Caoba and I spent many hours visiting with Max, learning about her practice, and hanging on to her every word, as she regaled us with stories of her life experiences.

Brandee Caoba curated an exhibition with great depth and movement, selecting several series of canvases and works on paper that reveal the intricacies and complexities of Max's work in a compelling and comprehensive way. *Endless Journey* is a testimonial to the great clarity of Max Cole's vision, her consistency and evolution as an artist, and her significant contribution to the legacy of abstraction.

PLATES

PLATE 1 **MICOUD**, 1979 acrylic on linen, 24 x 30 inches (61 x 76 cm)

FOLLOWING SPREAD

PLATE 2 **UNTITLED**, 1999 ink and acrylic on paper, 22 x 29¾ inches (56 x 76 cm)

PLATE 3 **SEPTEMBER 17, 1992**, 1992 ink, acrylic, washes on paper, 22¼ x 29½ inches (57 x 75 cm) Collection of Jeanne and Michael Klein

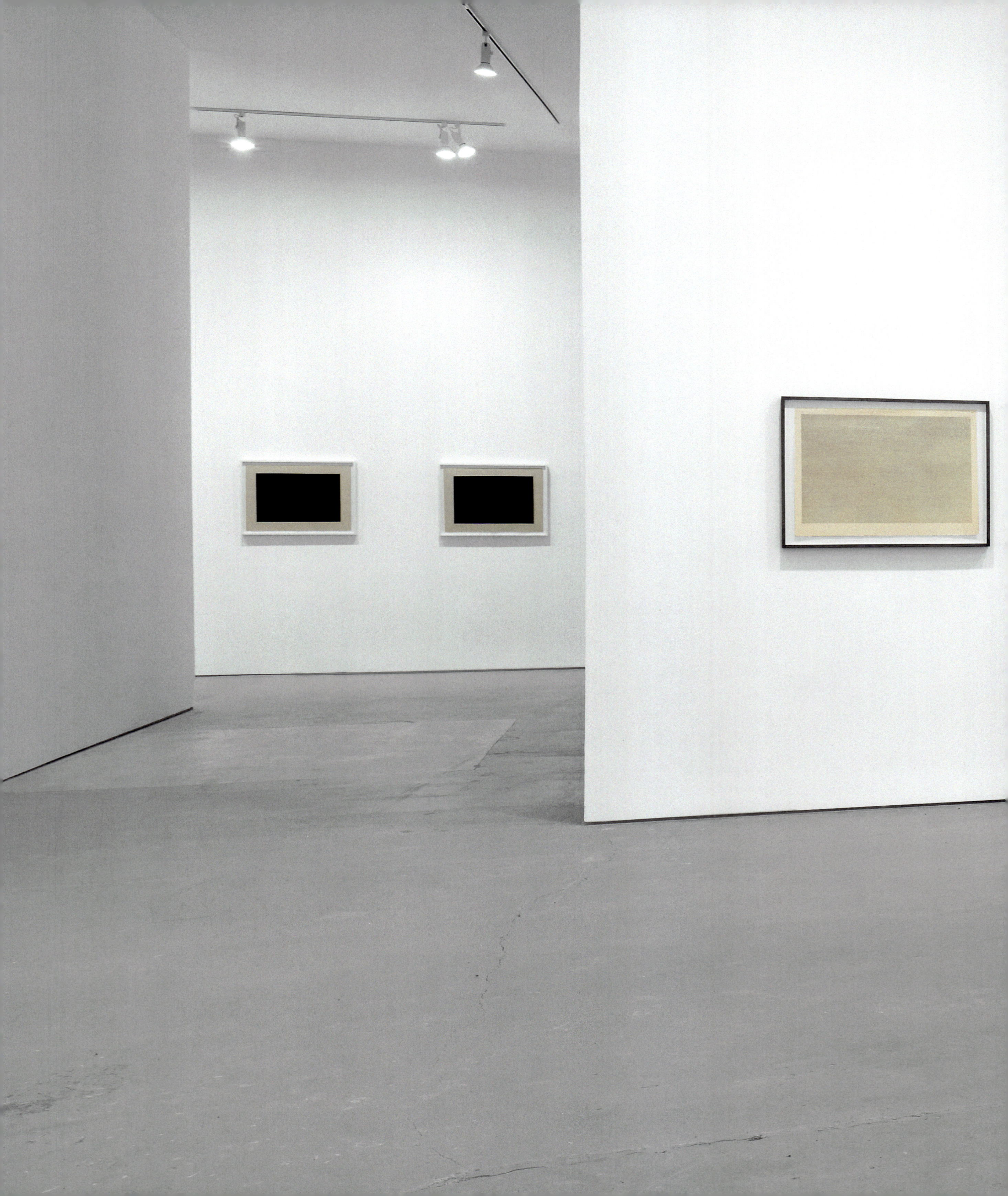

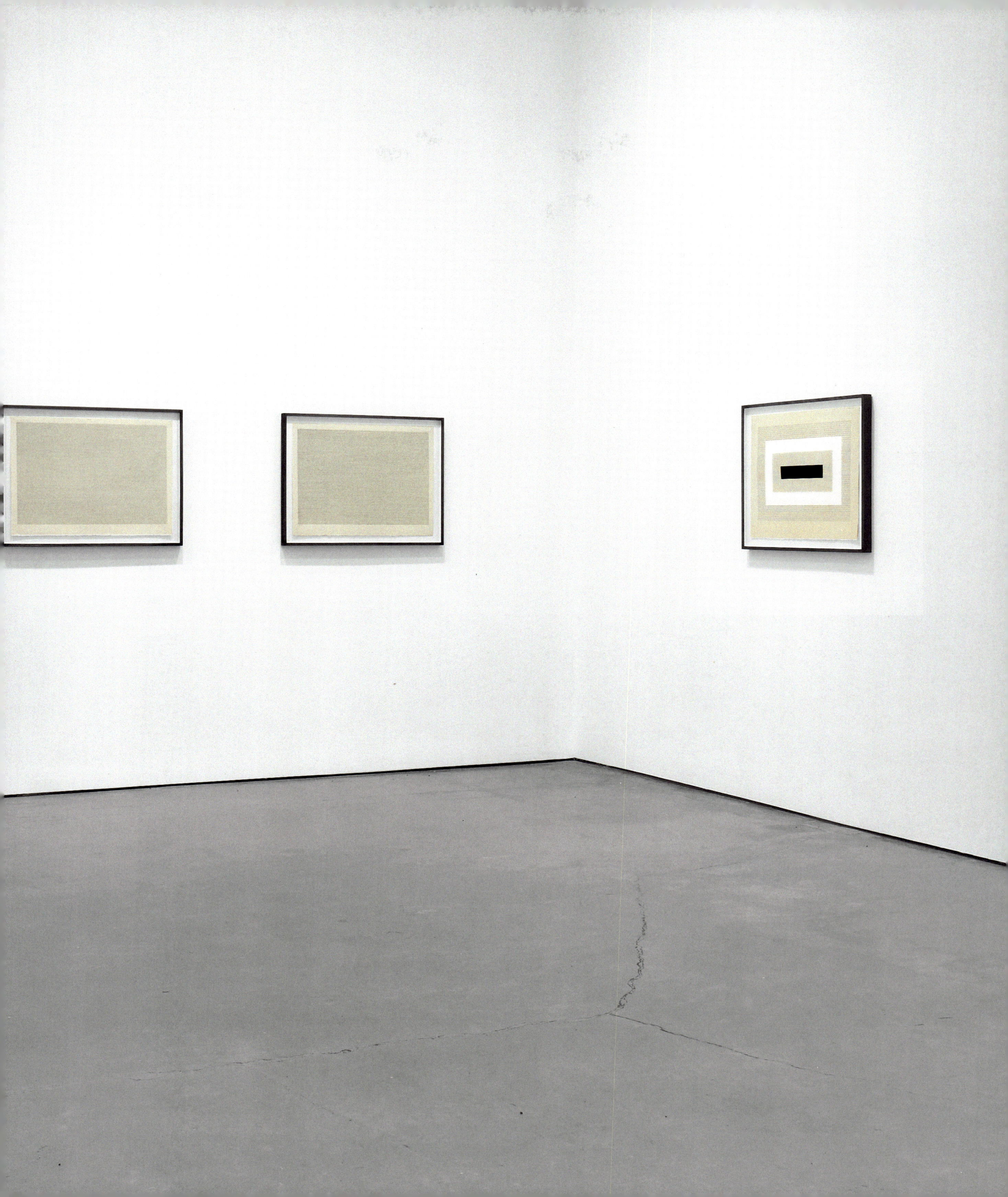

PLATE 4 **UNTITLED**, 1972 ink and acrylic on paper, 22 x 30 inches (56 x 76 cm) Collection of Jeanne and Michael Klein

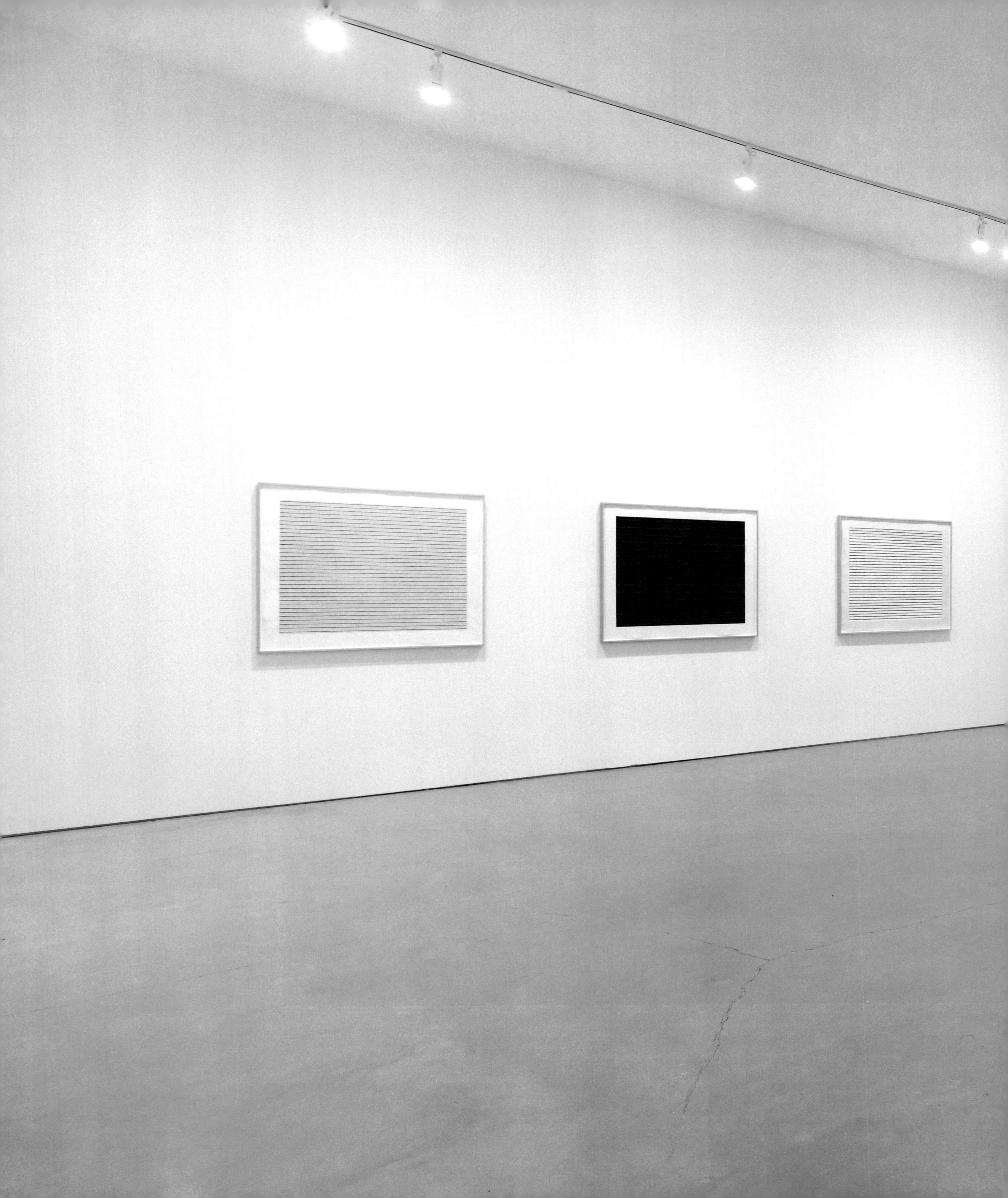

PLATE 5 **UNTITLED**, 2004 ink and acrylic on paper, 39¾ x 46 inches (101 x 117 cm)

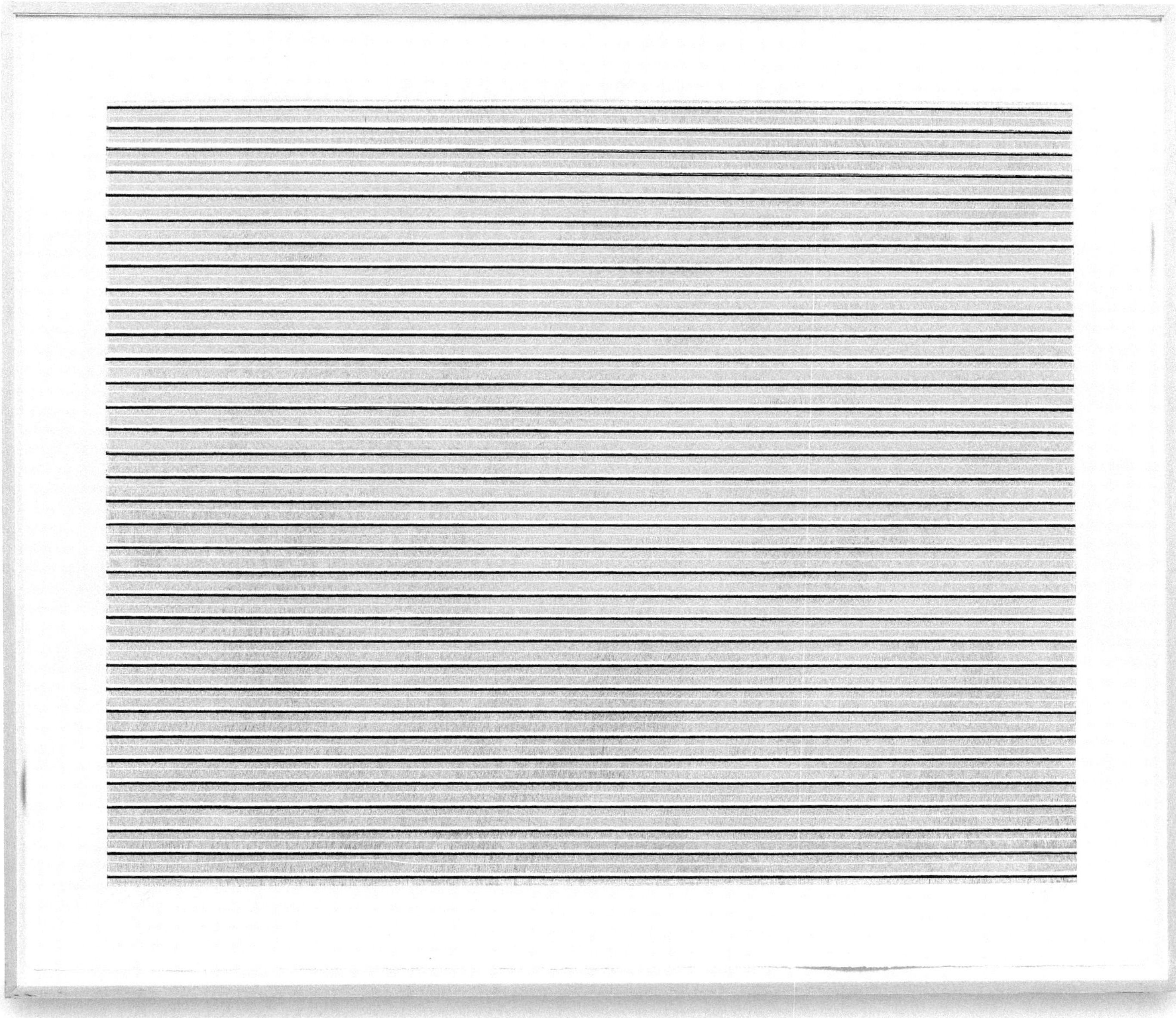

PLATE 6 **UNTITLED**, 2004 ink and acrylic on paper, 40 x 45¾ inches (102 x 116 cm)

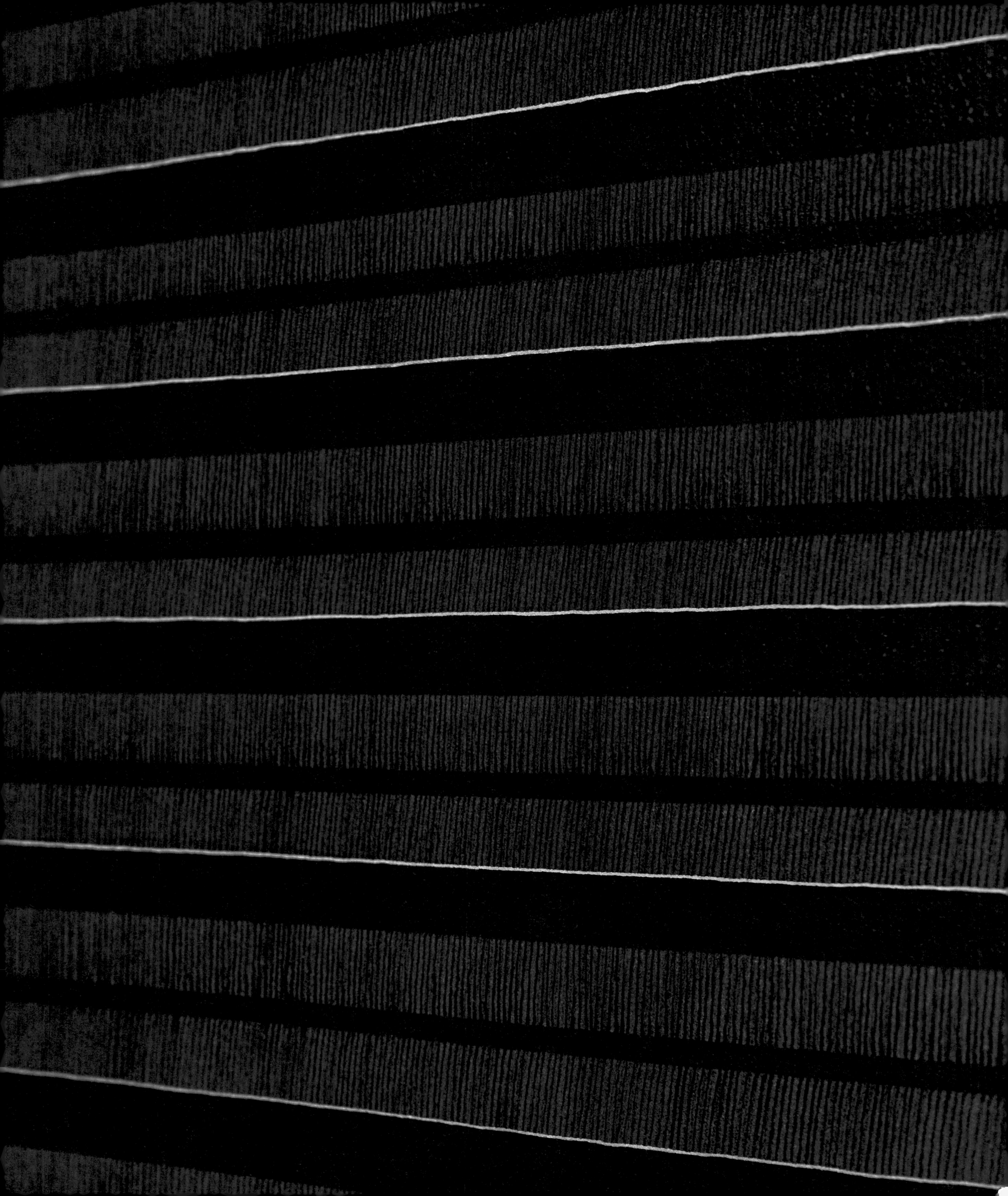

PLATE 7 **AUGUST #4**, 1988 ink and acrylic on paper, 46¾ x 71½ inches (116 x 182 cm) Private Collection

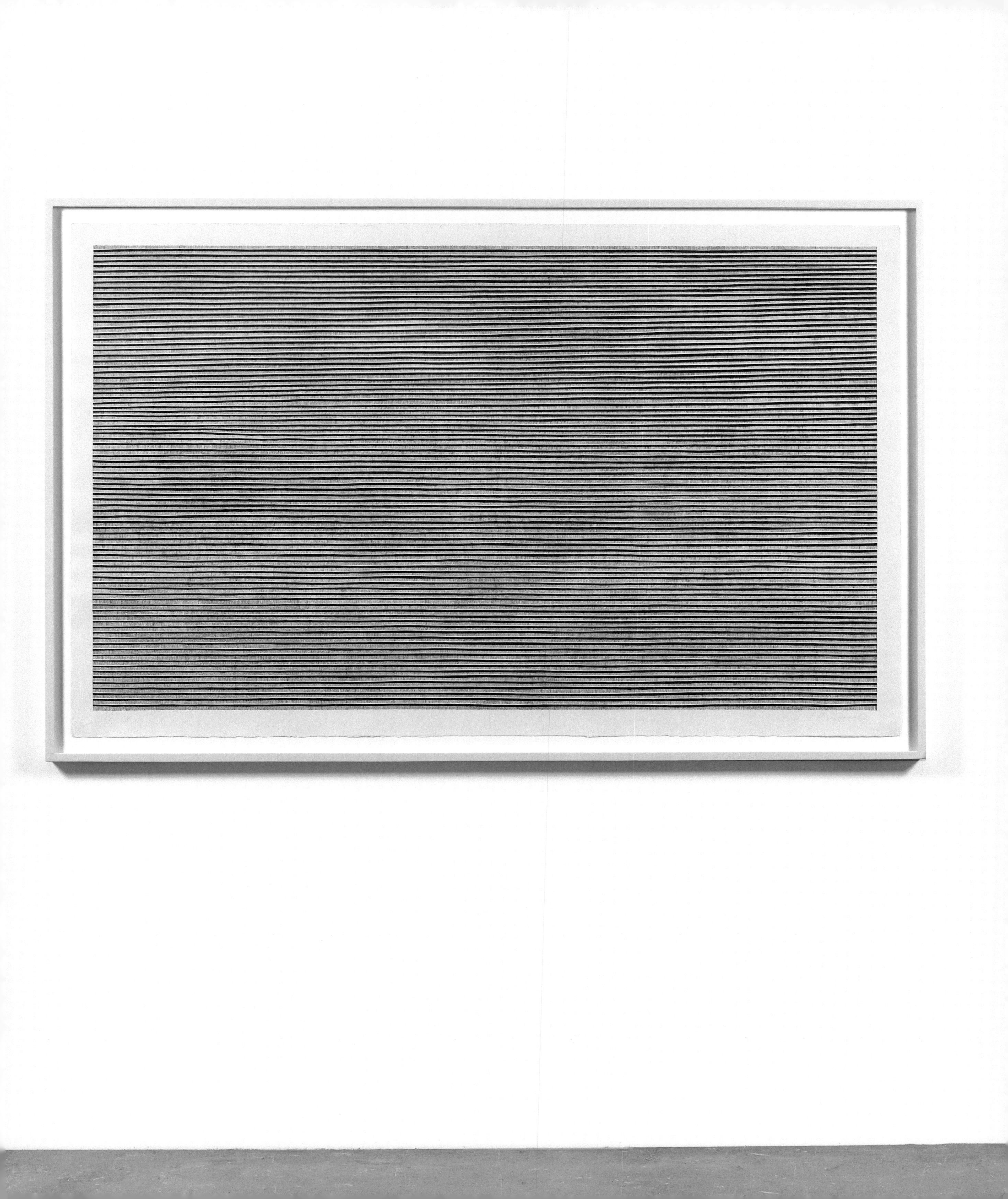

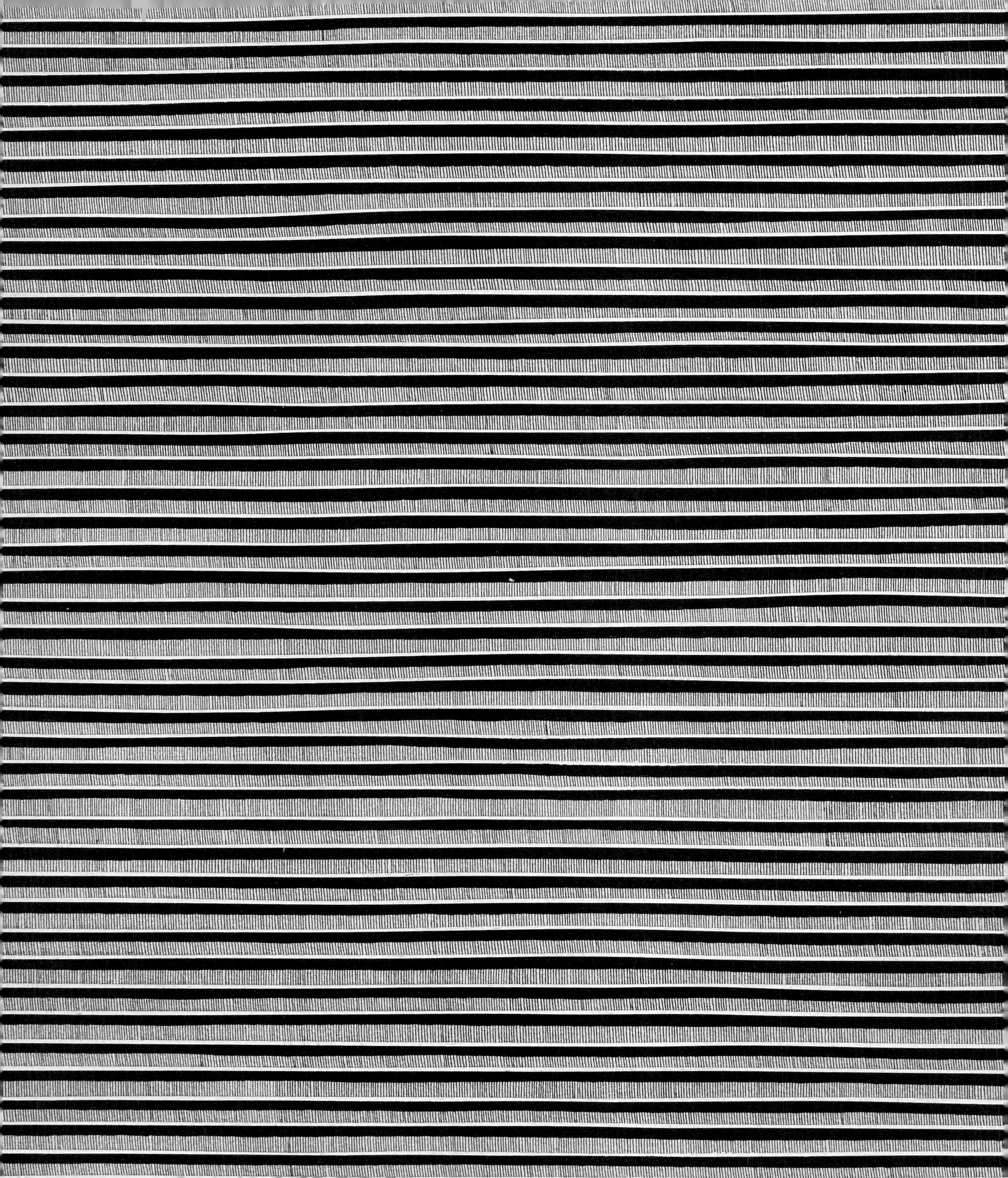

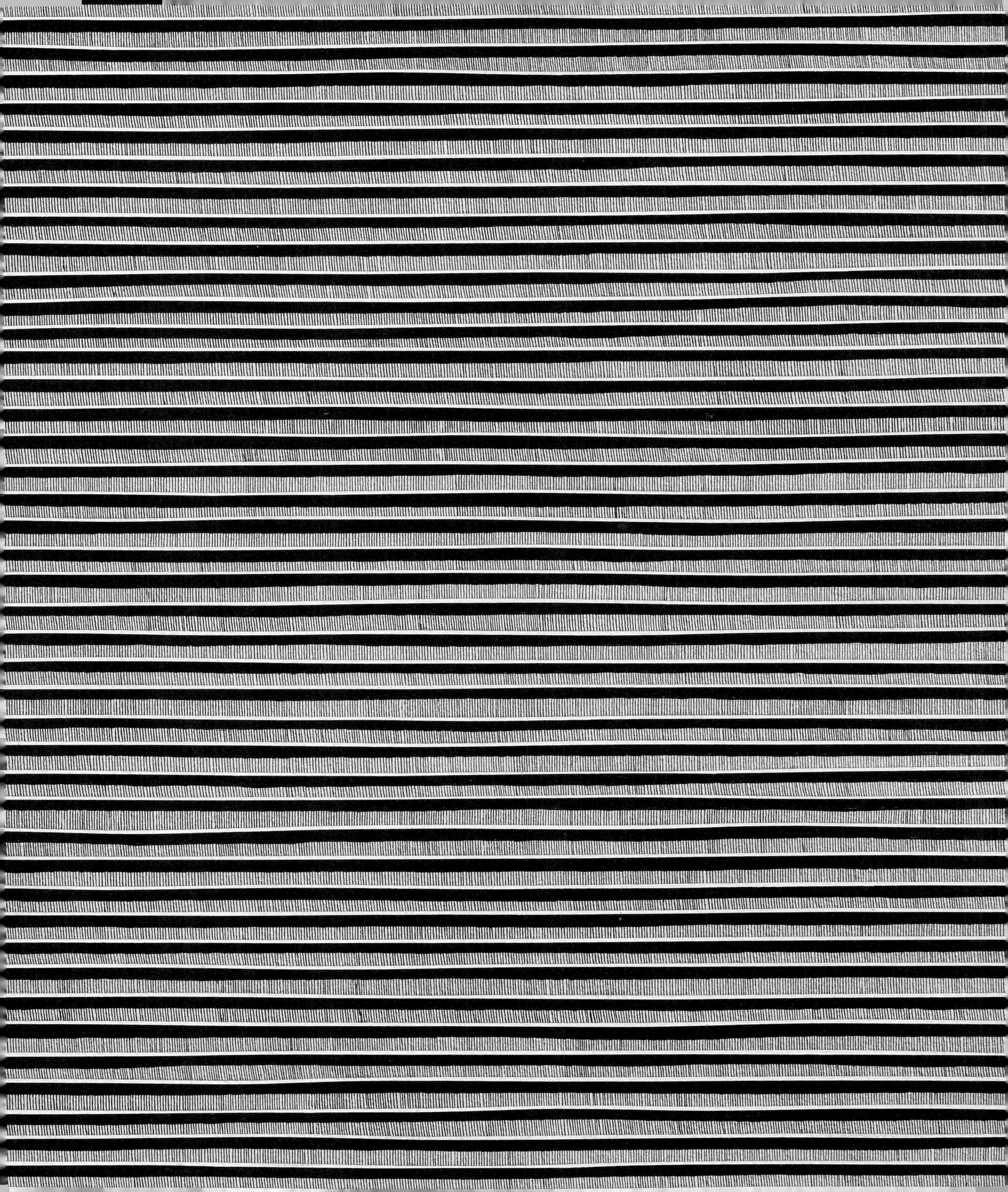

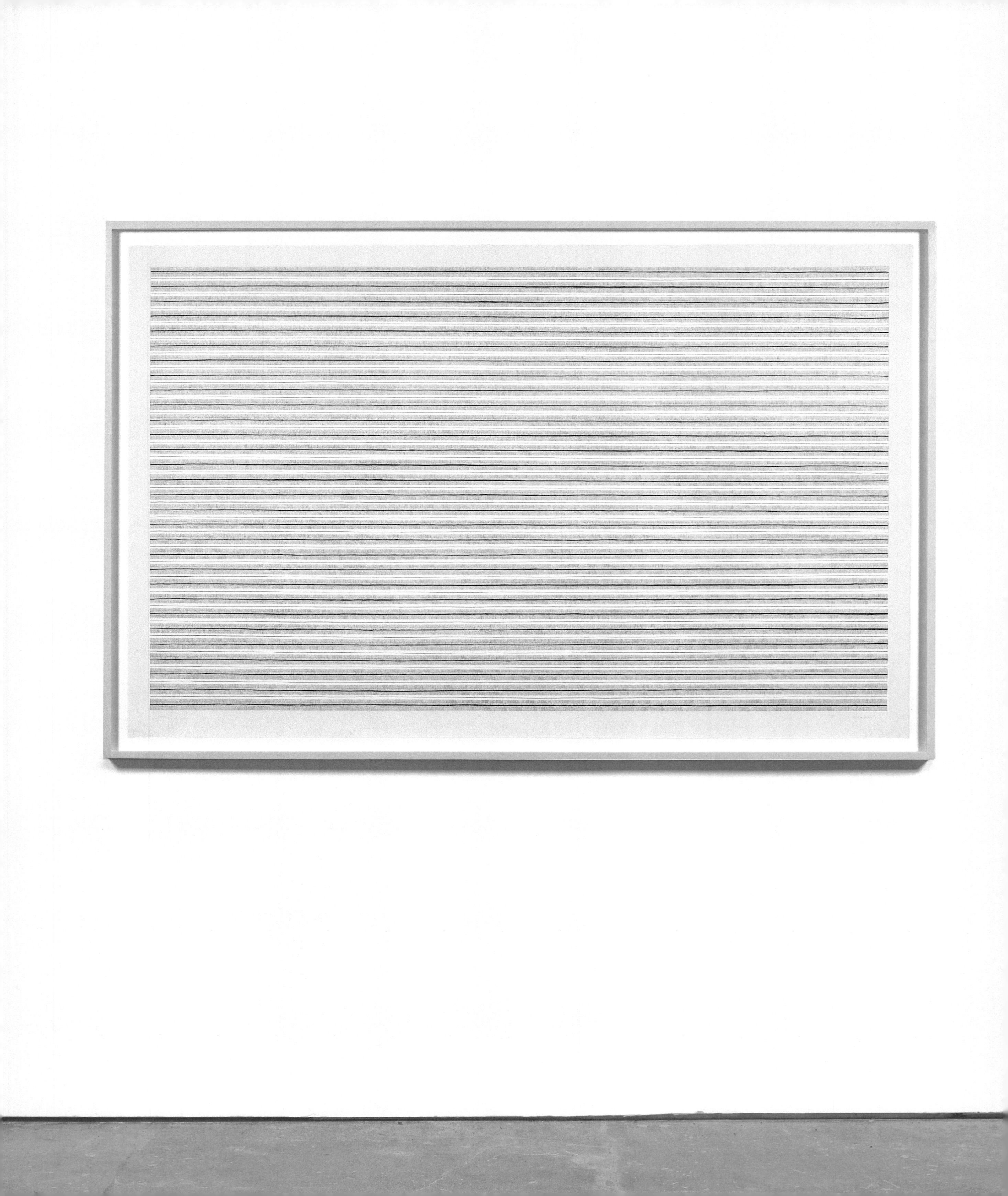

PLATE 8 **AUGUST #1**, 1988 ink and acrylic on paper, 46¾ x 71½ inches (116 x 182 cm) Private Collection

PLATE 9 **AUGUST #3**, 1988 ink and acrylic on paper, 46⅛ x 72 inches (117 x 183 cm) Private Collection

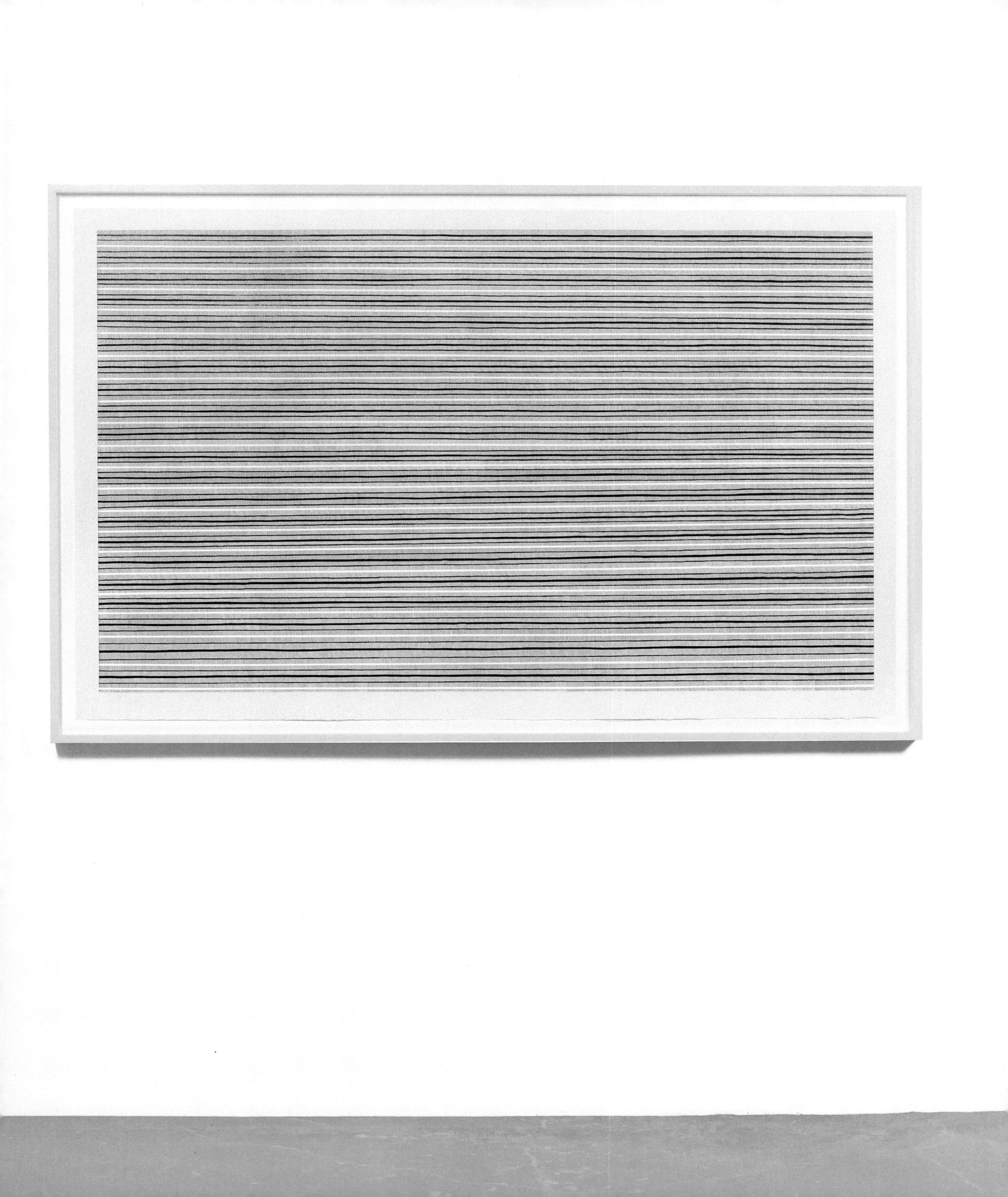

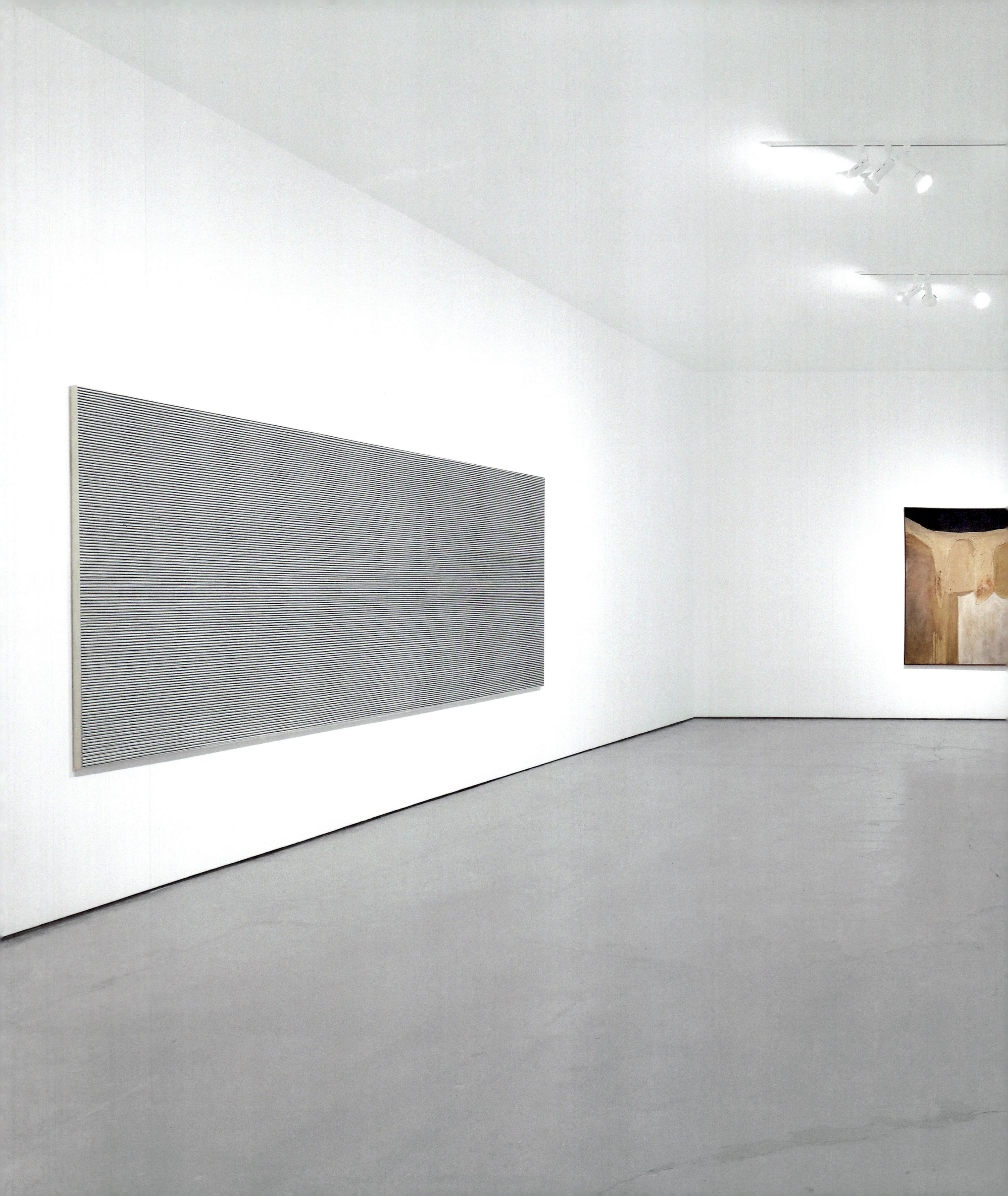

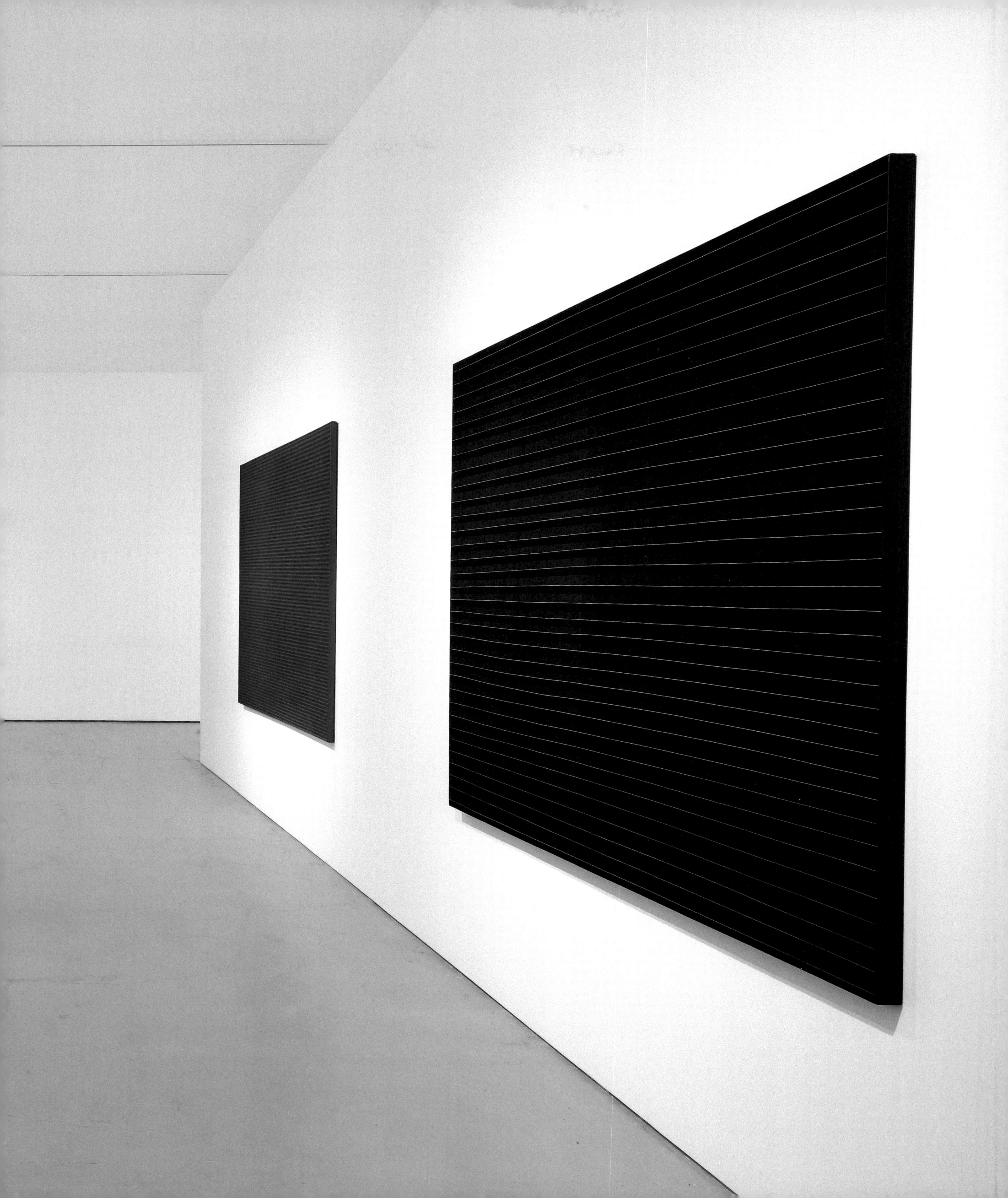

PLATE 10 **NOBLE NASSAU**, 1981 acrylic and ink on canvas, 68⅛ x 162¼ inches (172.7 x 411.5 cm) Collection of MOCA Los Angeles, gift of Joan and Melanie Borinstein

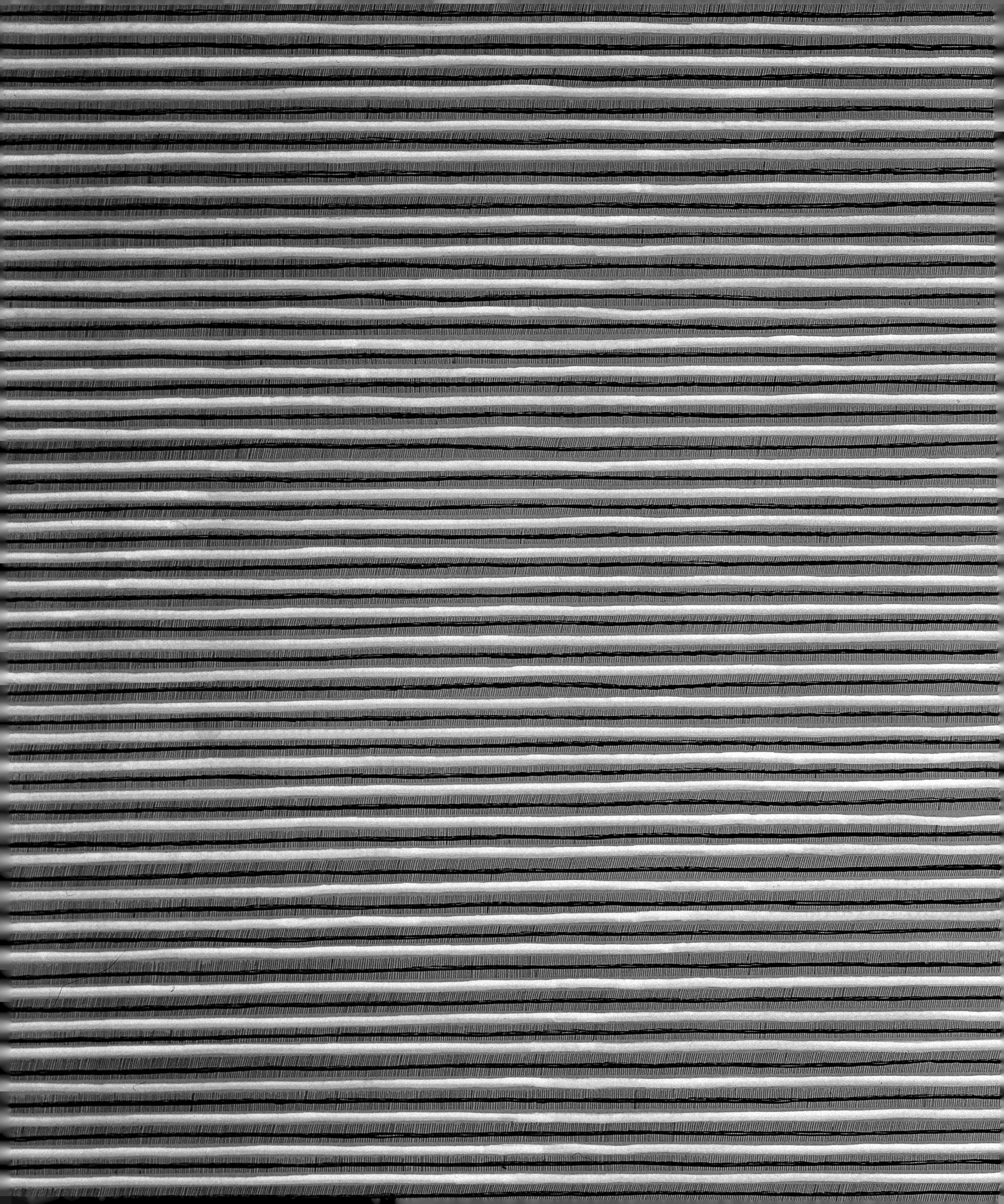

PLATE 11 **SHAWNEE**, 1979 acrylic on linen, 68 x 81 inches (173 x 206 cm)

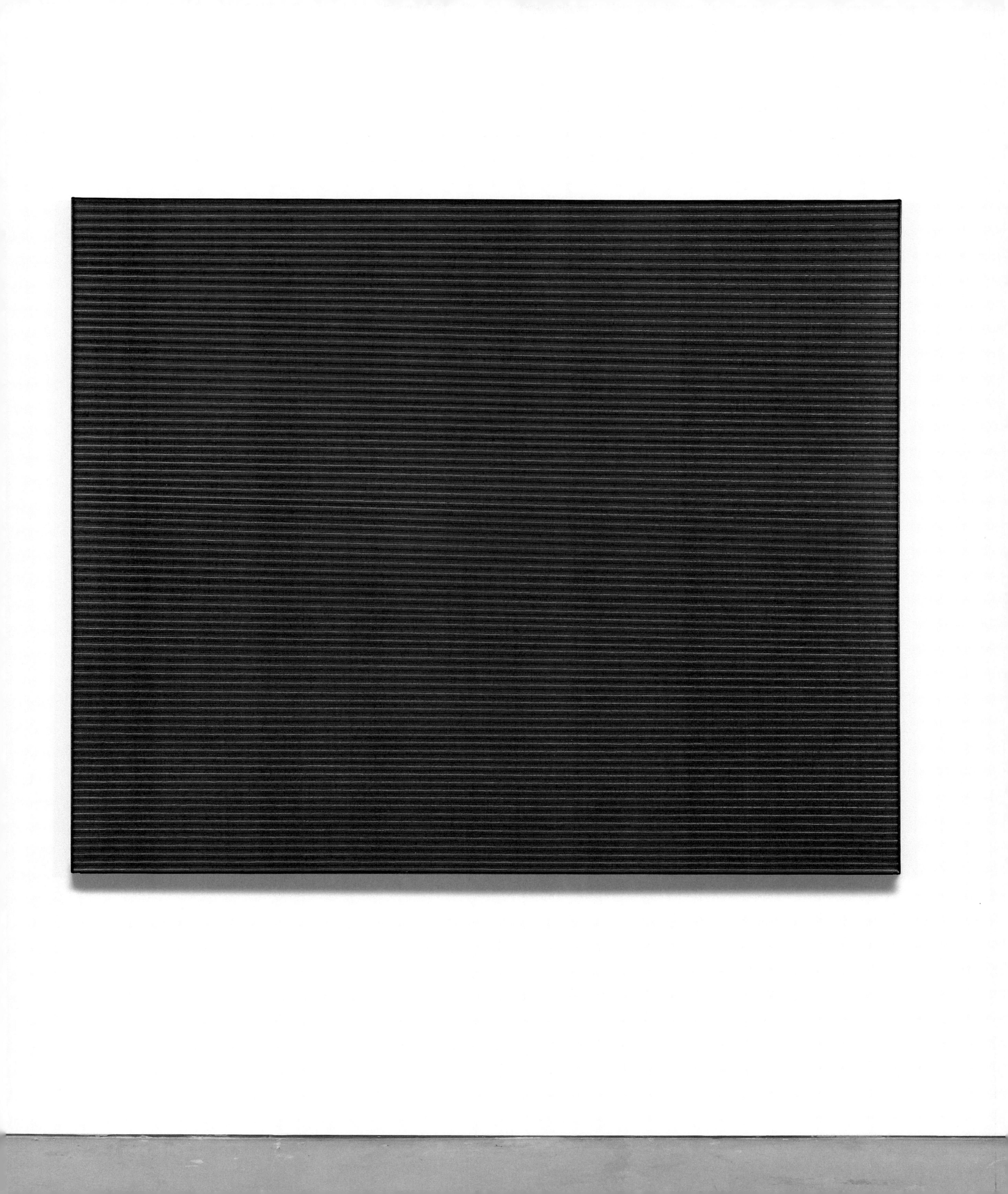

PLATE 12 **WOLF TRAP**, 2006 acrylic on linen, 68 x 80 inches (173 x 203 cm)

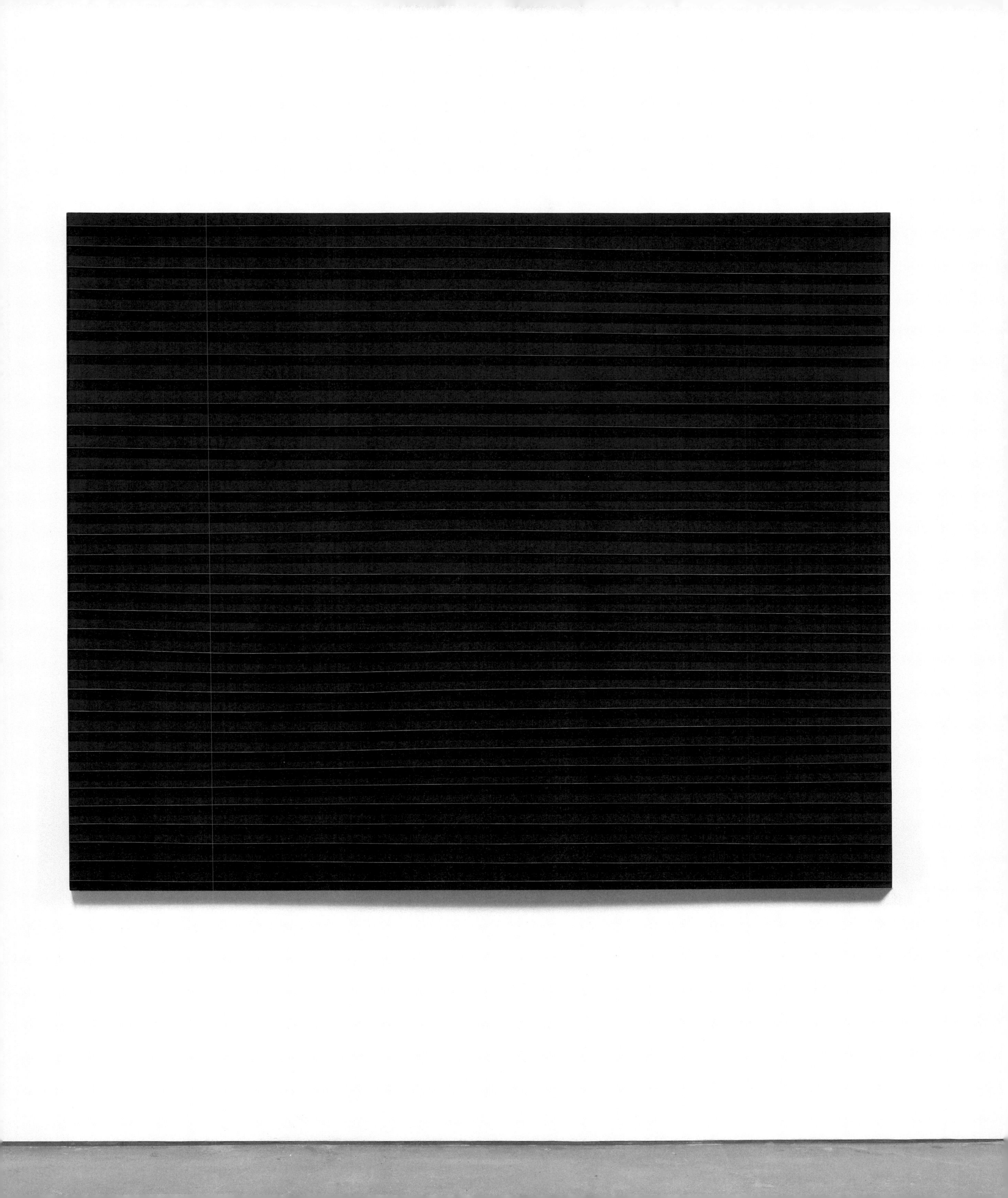

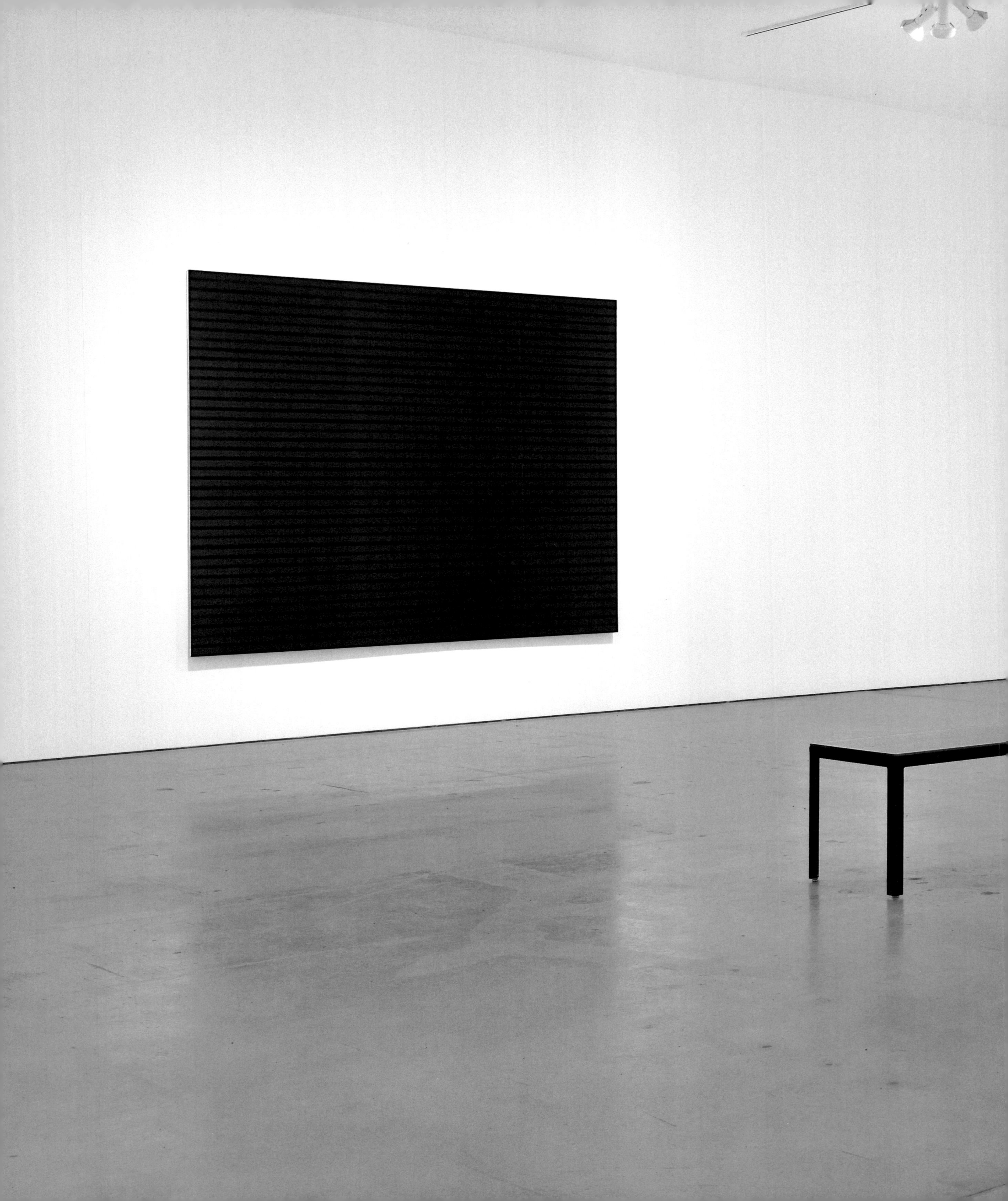

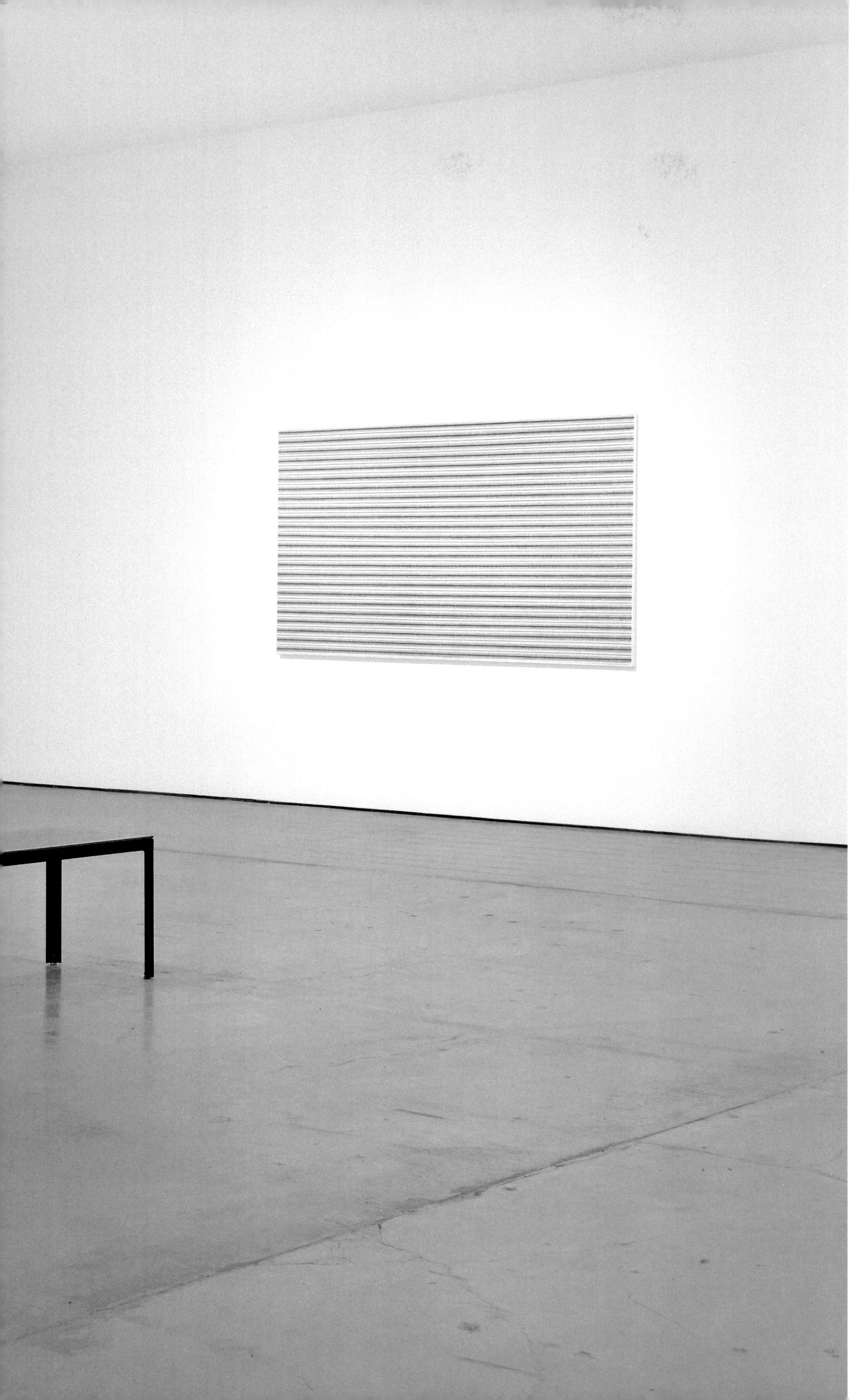

PLATE 13 **RED**, 1986 acrylic on linen, 79 x 92 inches (201 x 234 cm) Collection of Henry R. Muñoz III

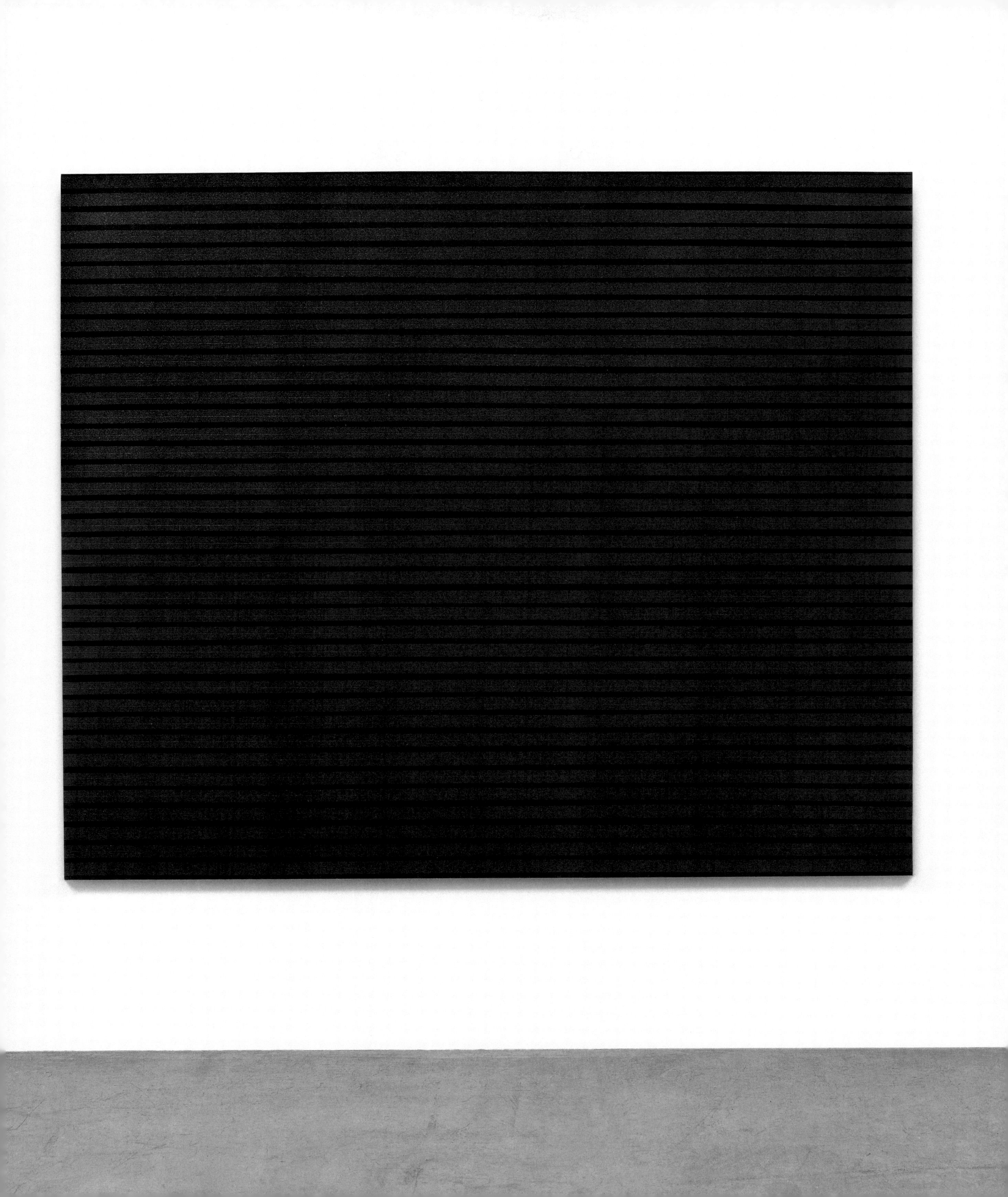

PLATE 14 **CHUAR II**, 1986 acrylic on linen, 52 x 92 inches (132 x 234 cm)

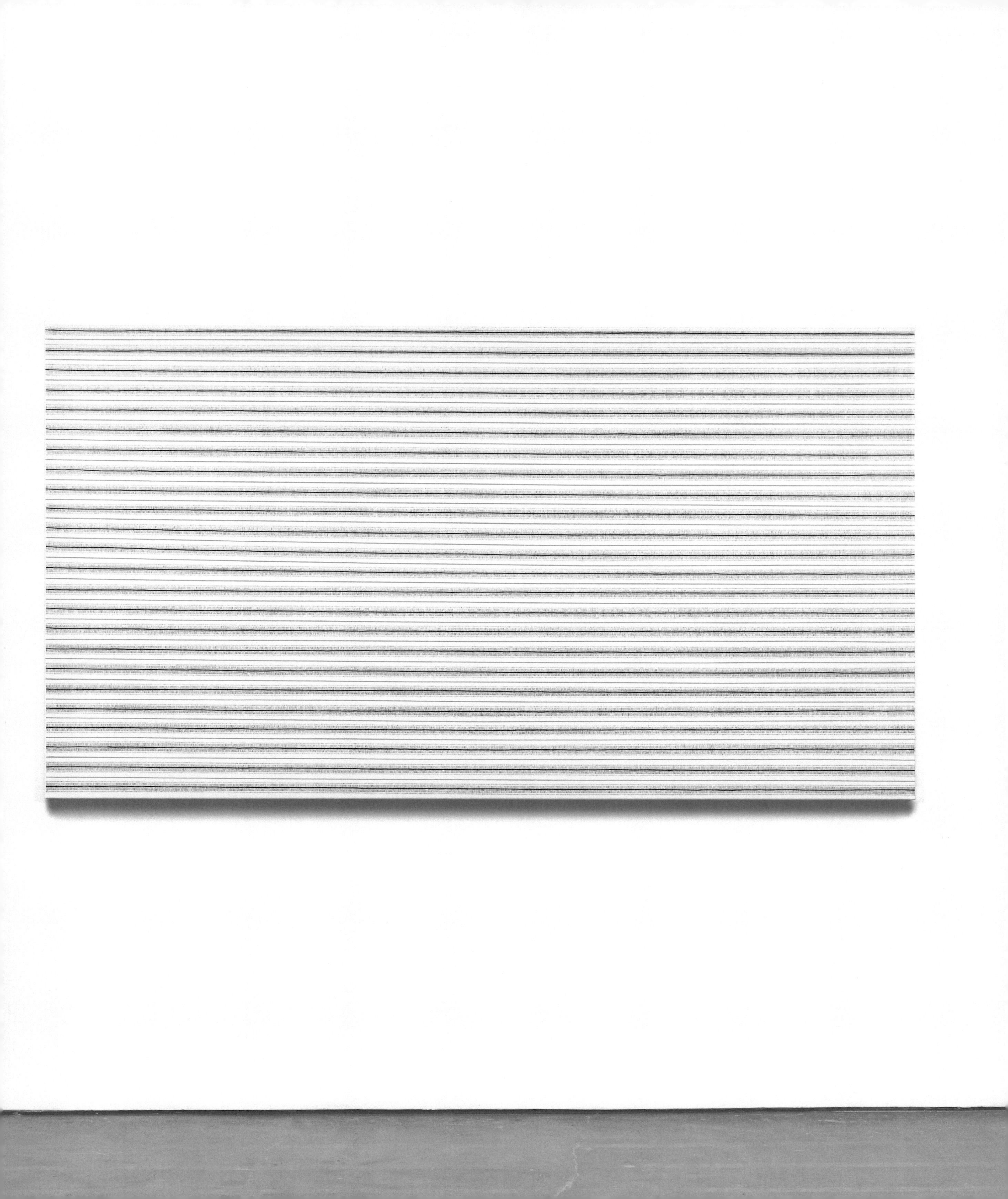

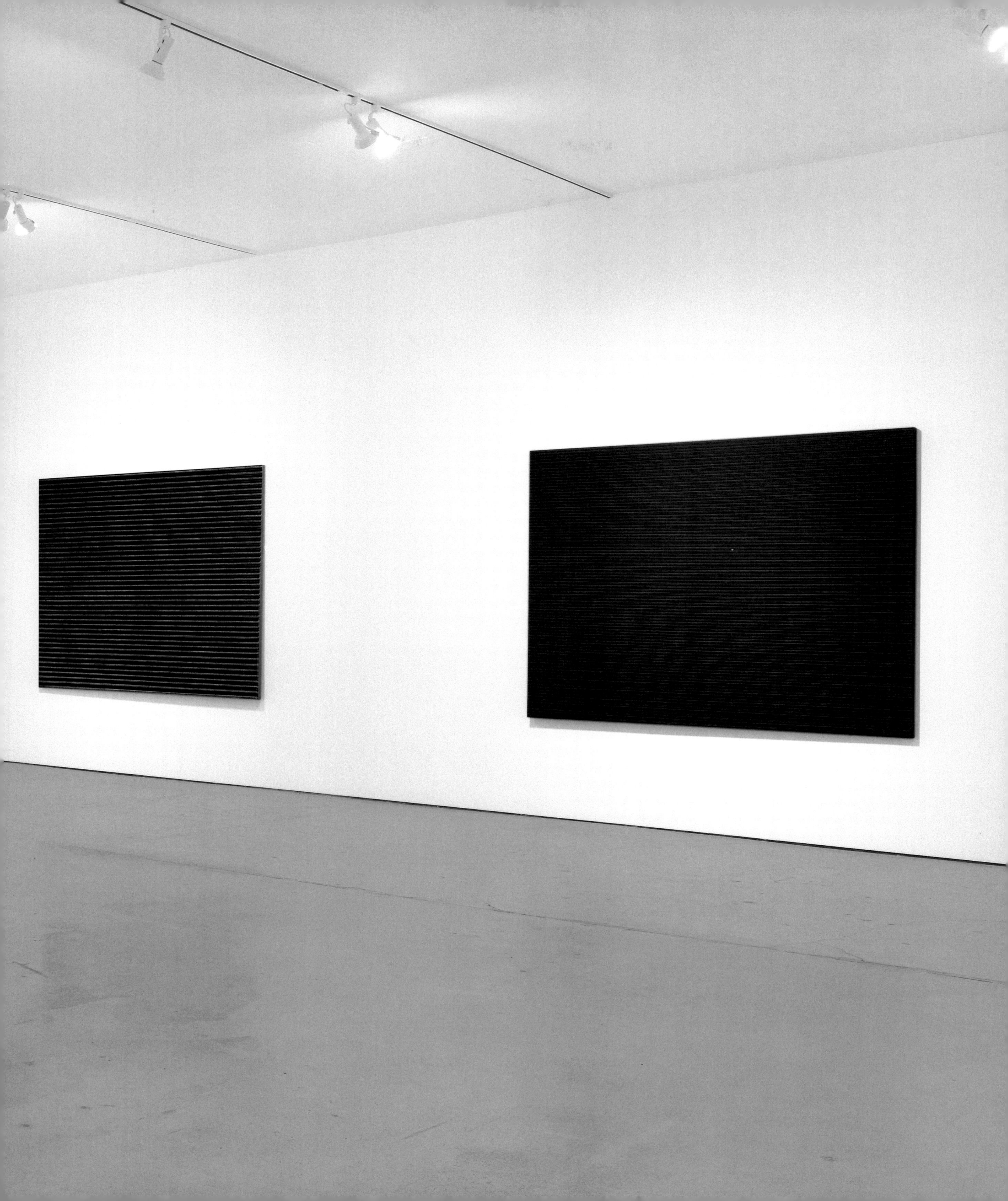

PLATE 15 **SHINUMO**, 1984 acrylic on canvas, 52 x 92 inches (132 x 234 cm)

FOLLOWING SPREAD

PLATE 16 **MESA**, 2003 acrylic on linen, 68 x 80 inches (173 x 203 cm) The Nelsen Collection

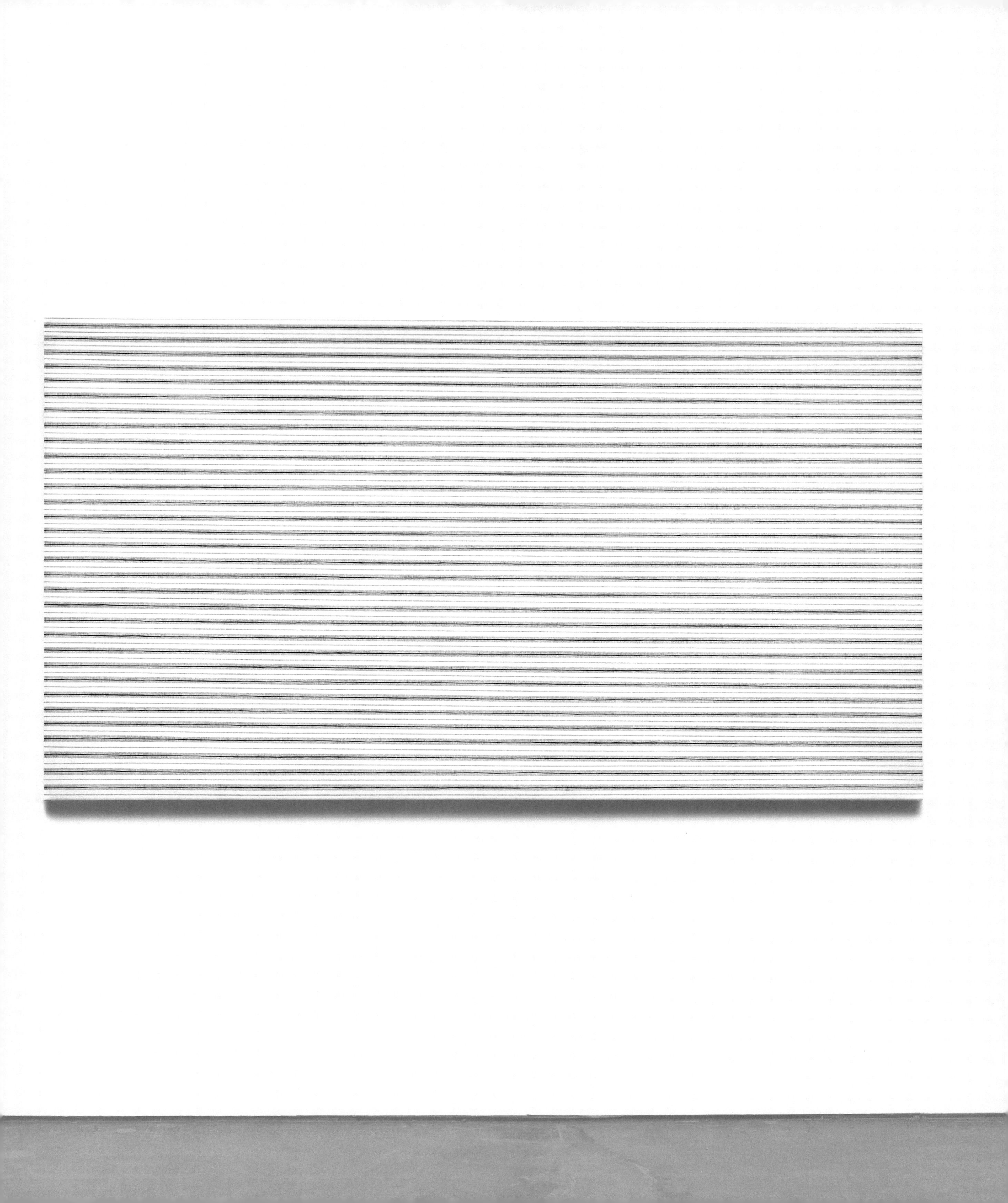

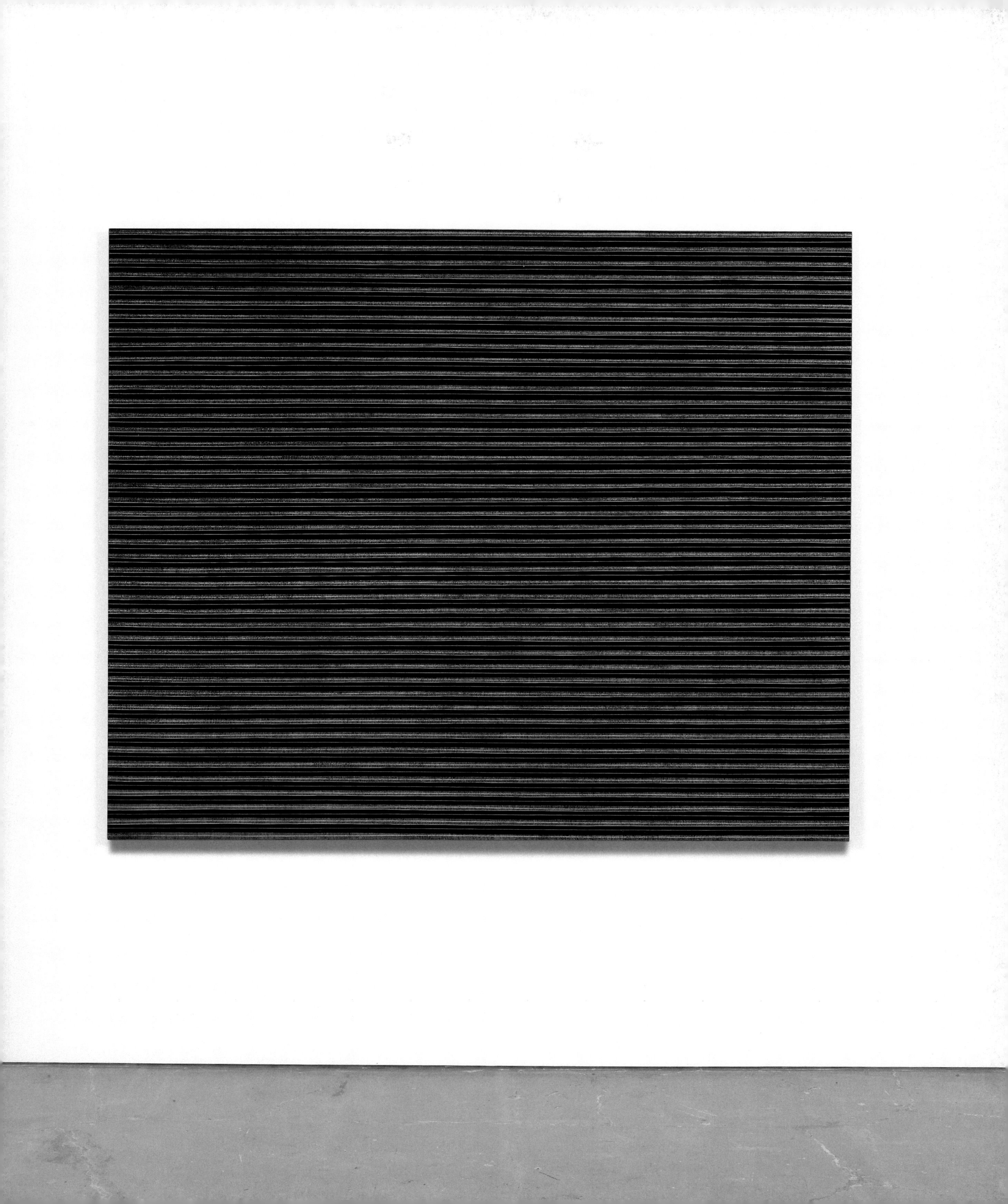

PLATE 17 **RACER**, 2000 acrylic on linen, 68 x 81 inches (173 x 206 cm)

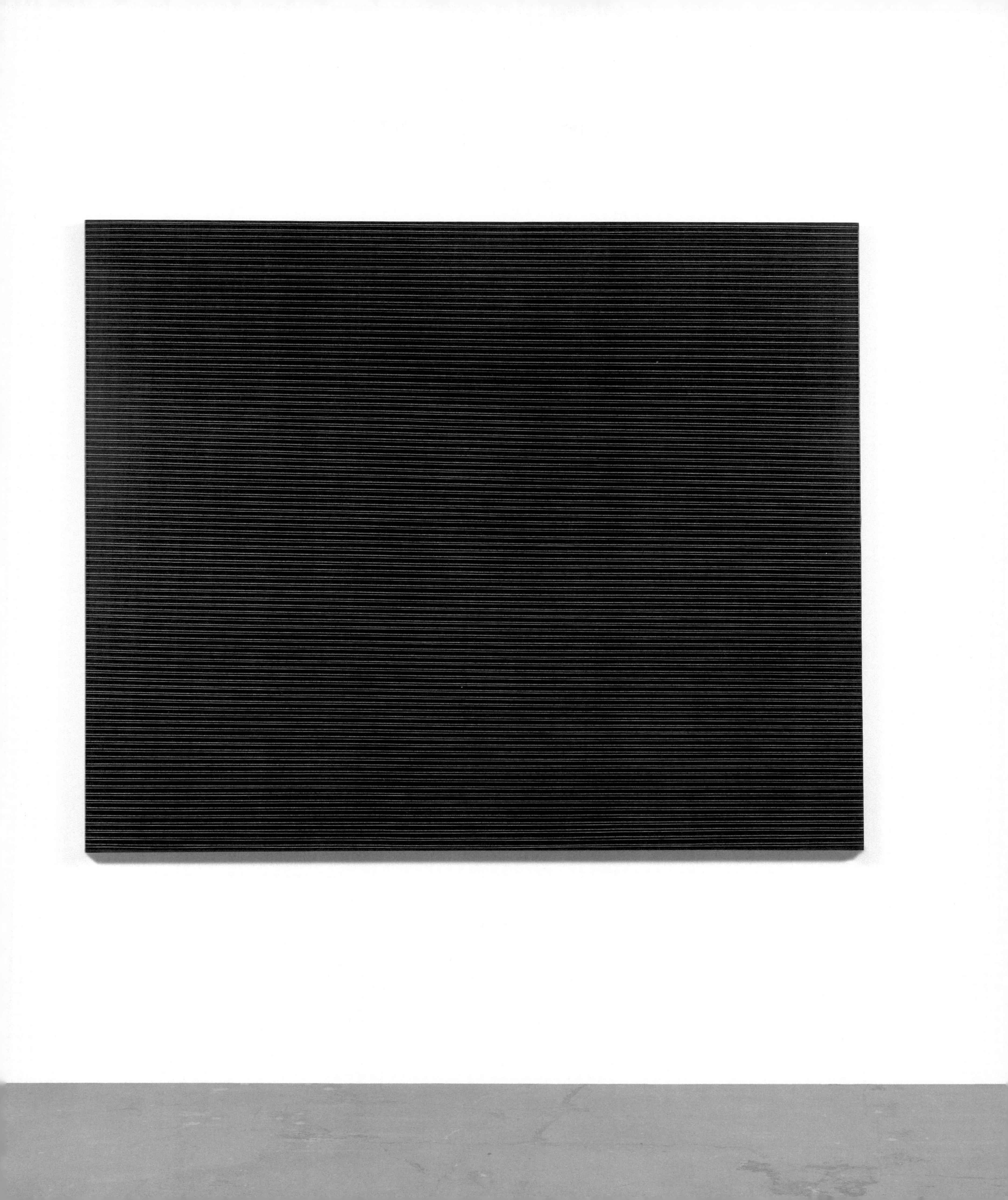

PLATE 18 **TESUQUE**, 2000 acrylic on linen, 52 x 62 inches (132 x 157 cm) Collection of Jayne and Michael Flinn

PLATE 19 **TITANIA, 2003** acrylic on linen, 68 x 80 inches (173 x 203 cm) Collection of Johanna and Lief Rosenblatt

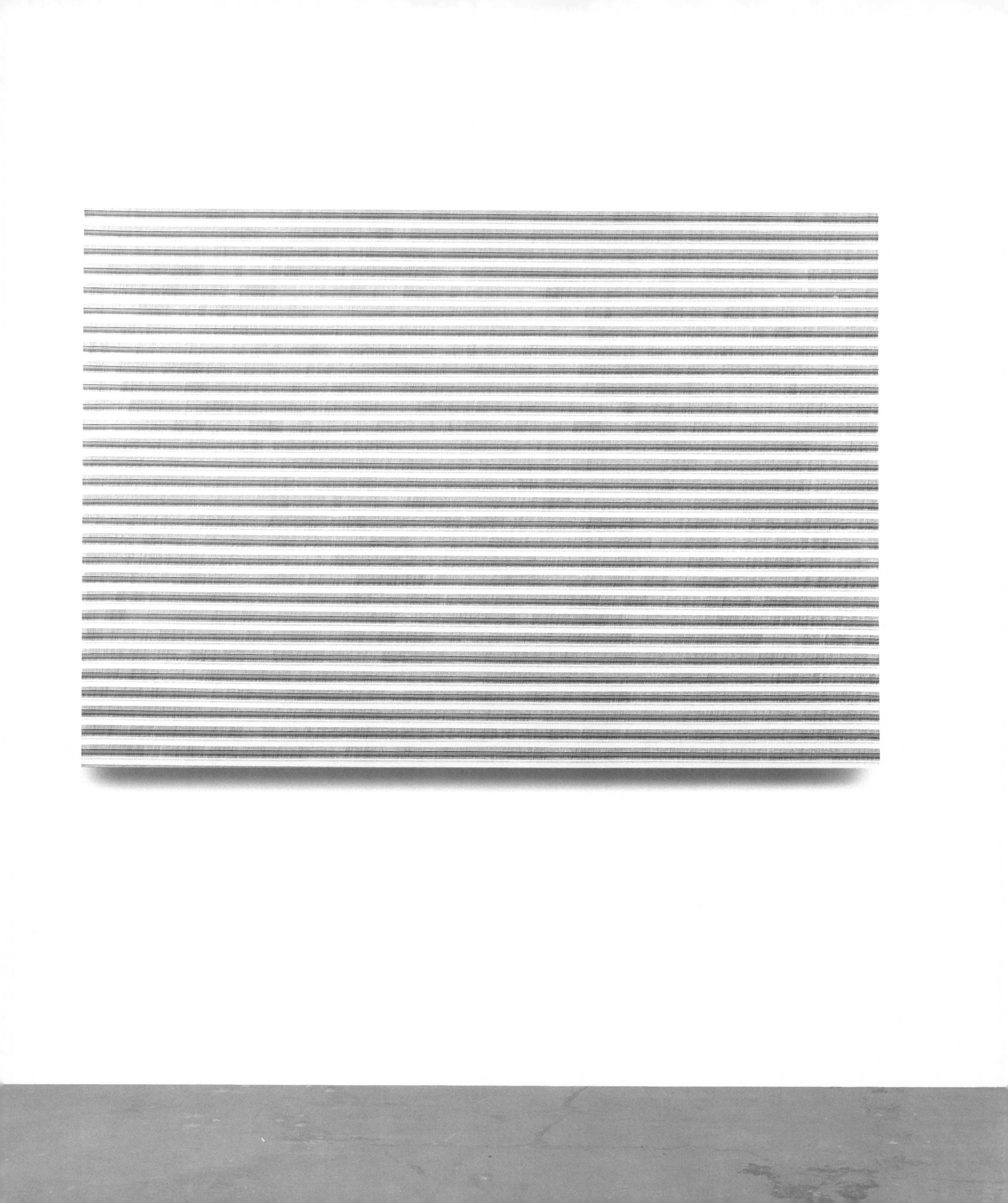

PLATE 20 **EBONY/IVORY II**, 2022 acrylic on linen, 36 x 36 inches (91 x 91 cm) Collection of Geraldine and Matthew Hooks

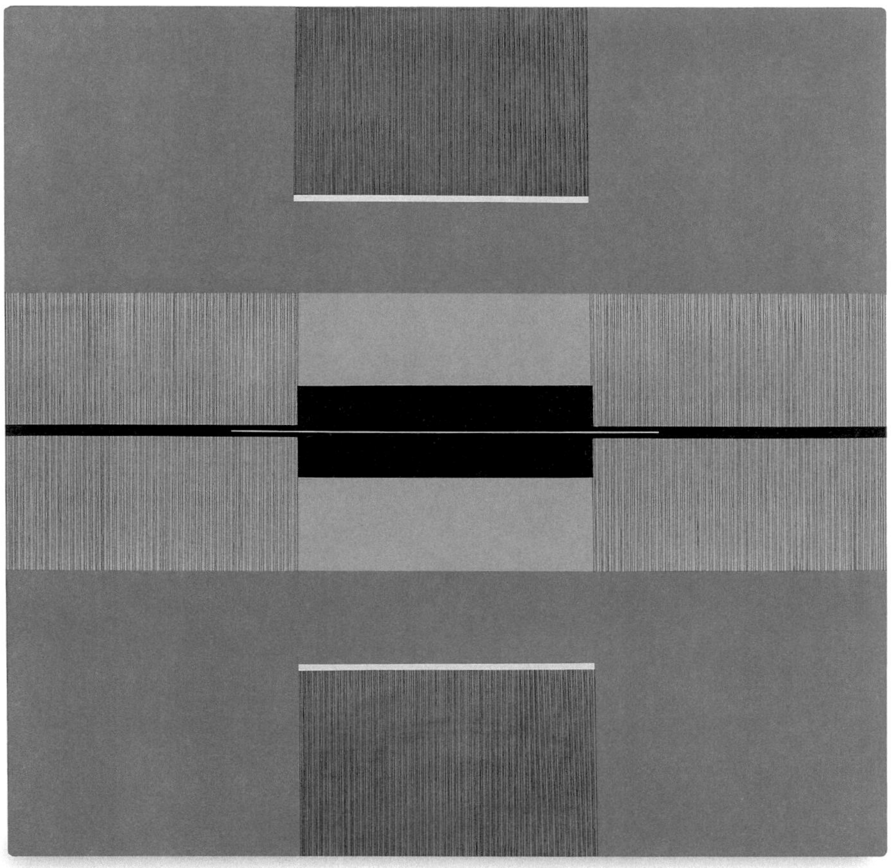

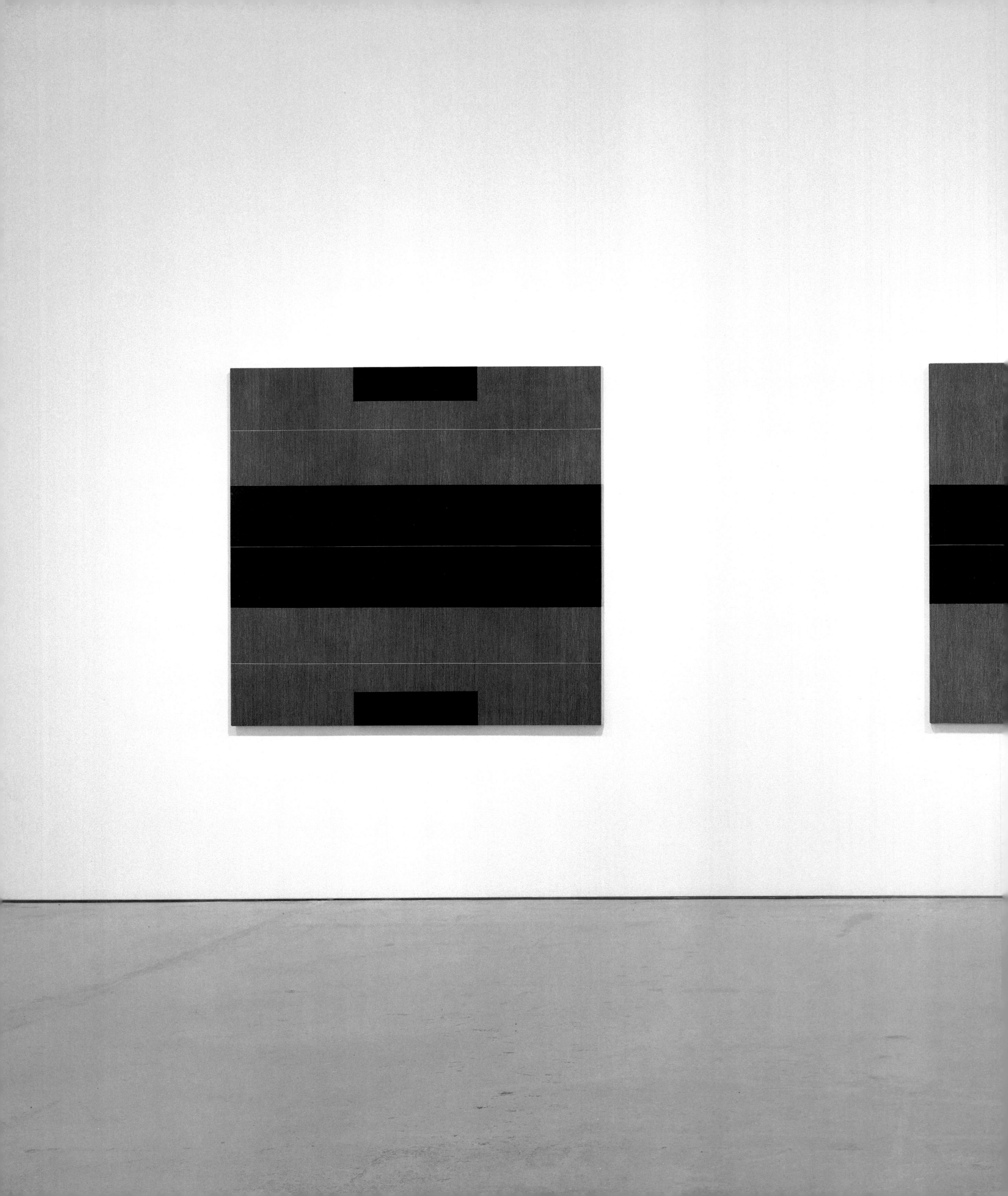

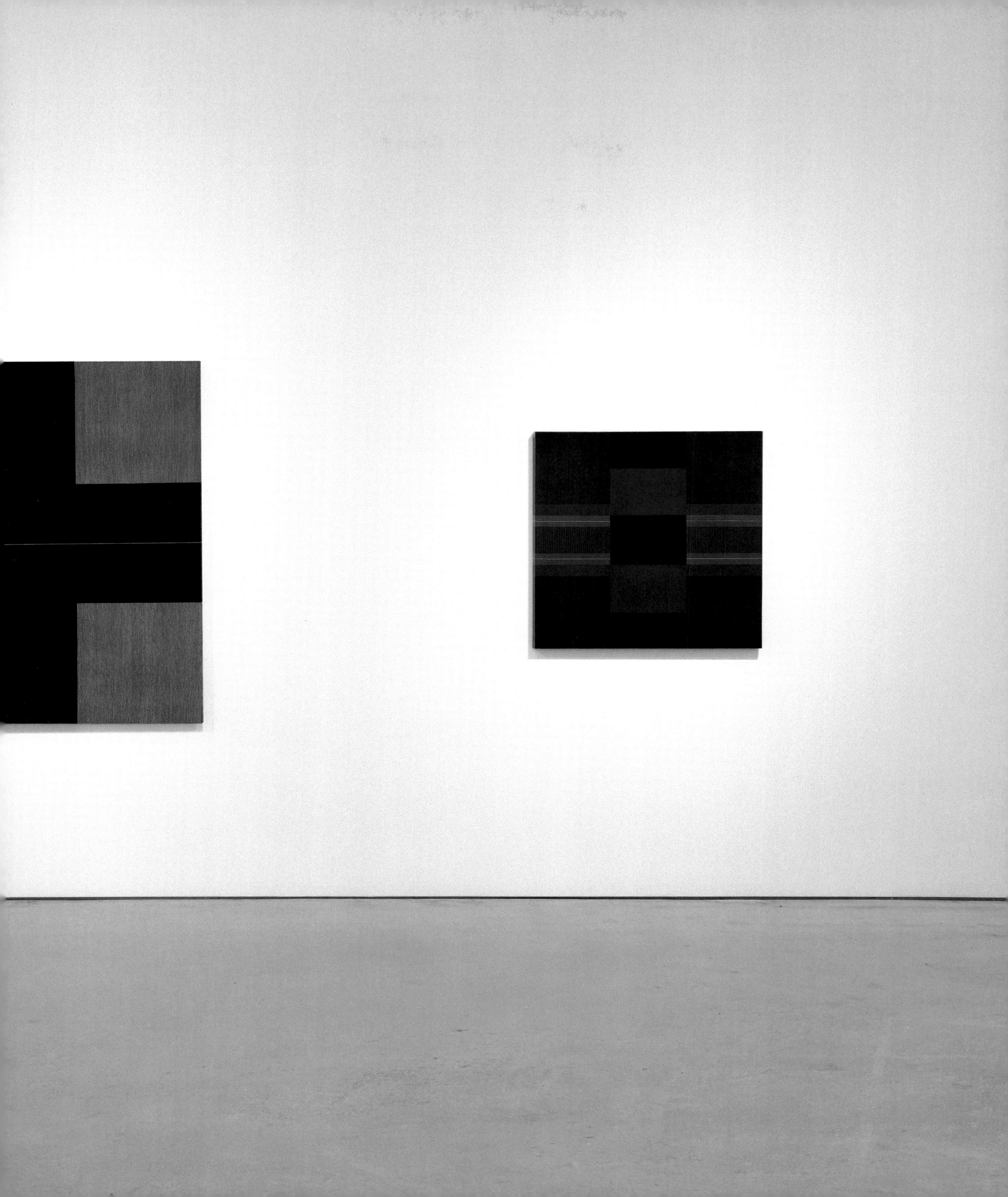

PLATE 21 **GREEK CROSS V**, 2015 acrylic on linen, 60 x 60 inches (152 x 152 cm) Tia Collection

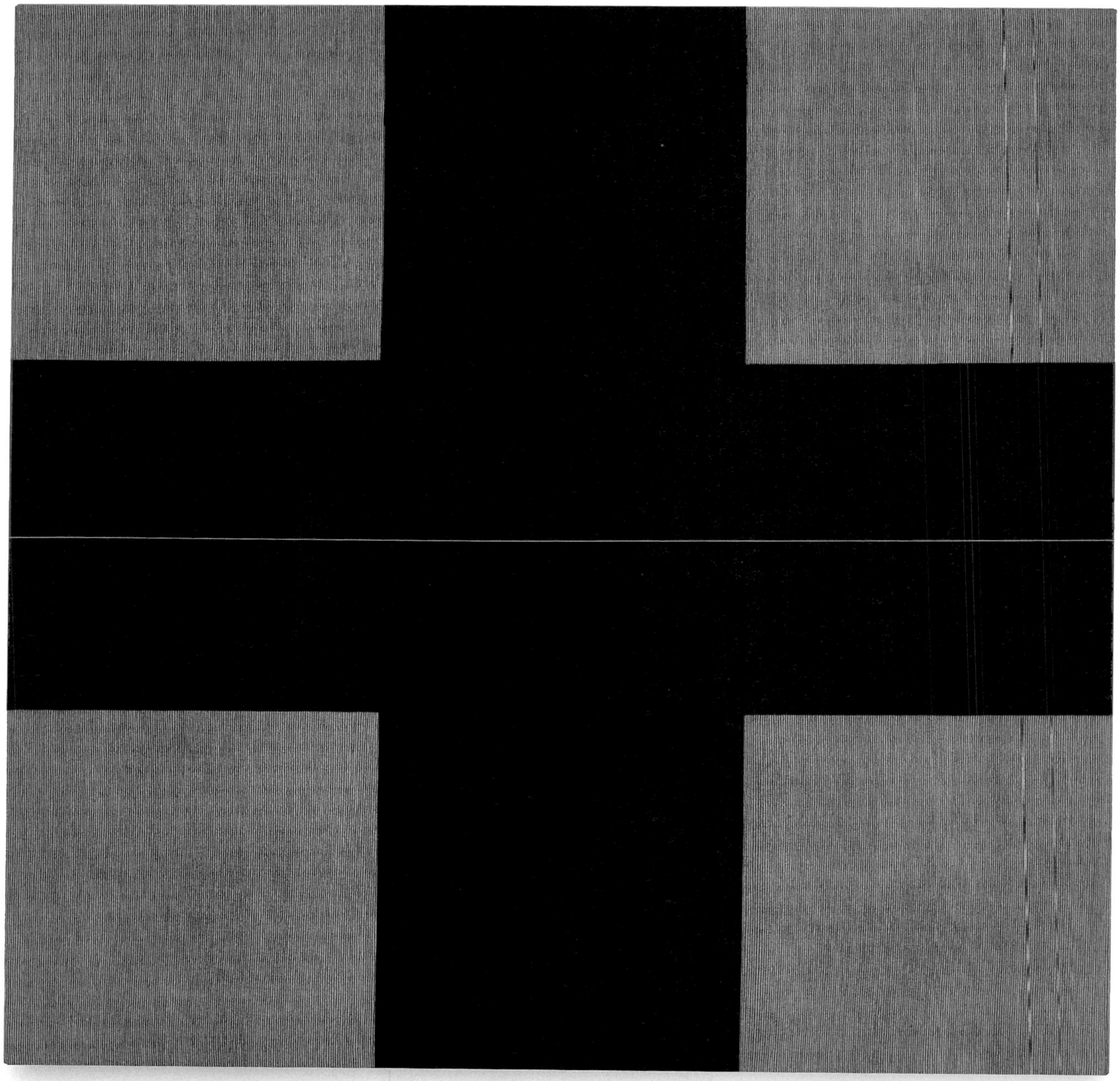

PLATE 22 **GREEK CROSS III**, 2015 acrylic on linen, 60 x 60 inches (152 x 152 cm) Tia Collection

PLATE 23 **EBONY/IVORY VIII**, 2022 acrylic on linen, 36 x 36 inches (91 x 91 cm) Collection of Museum Art.Plus, Donaueschingen, Germany

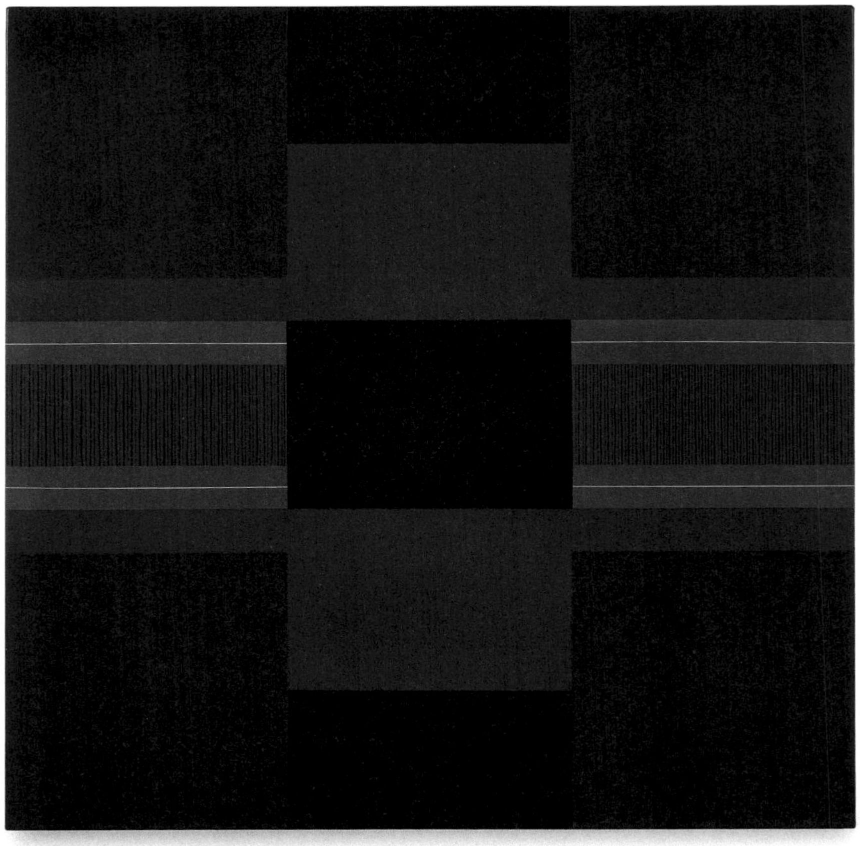

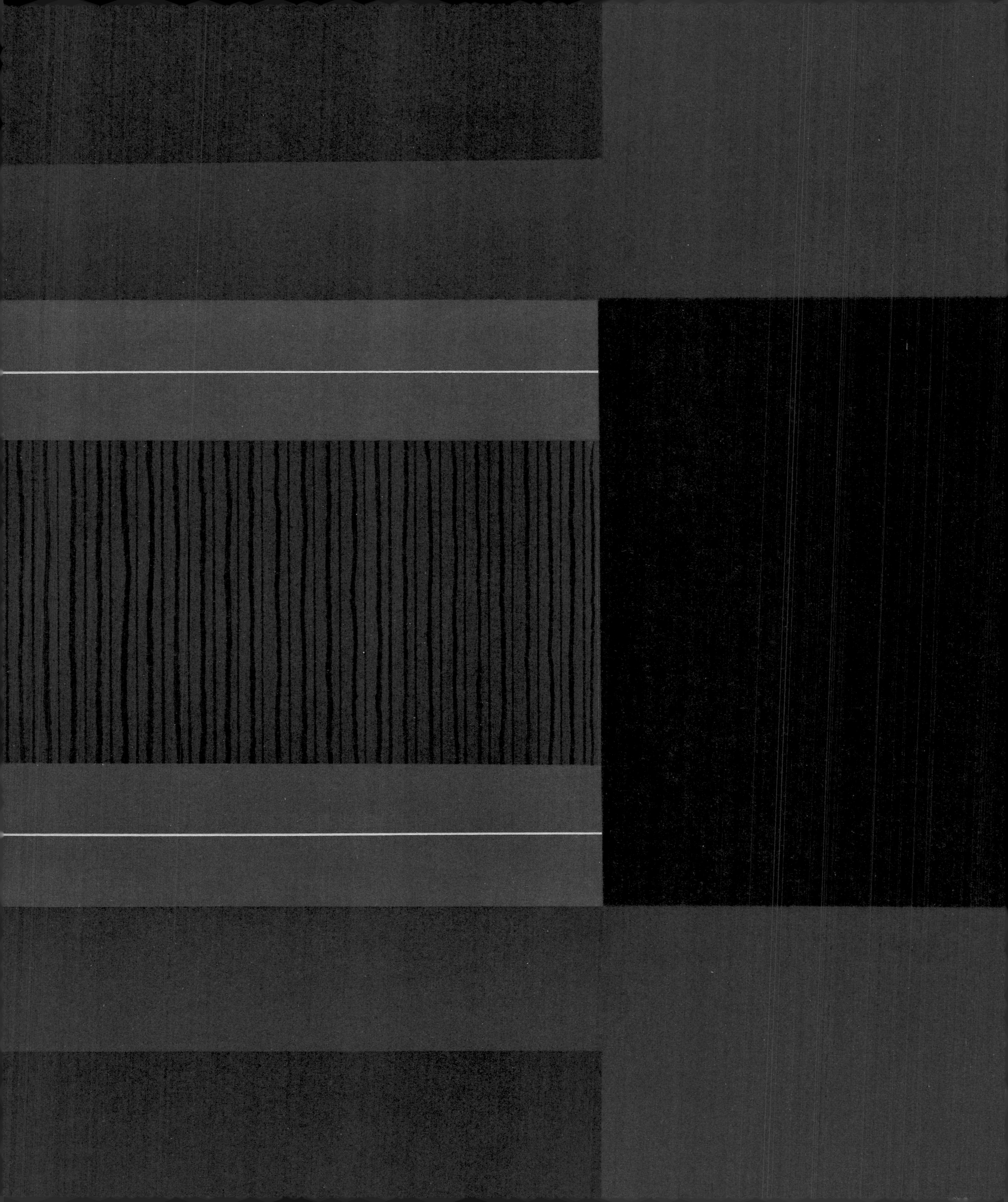

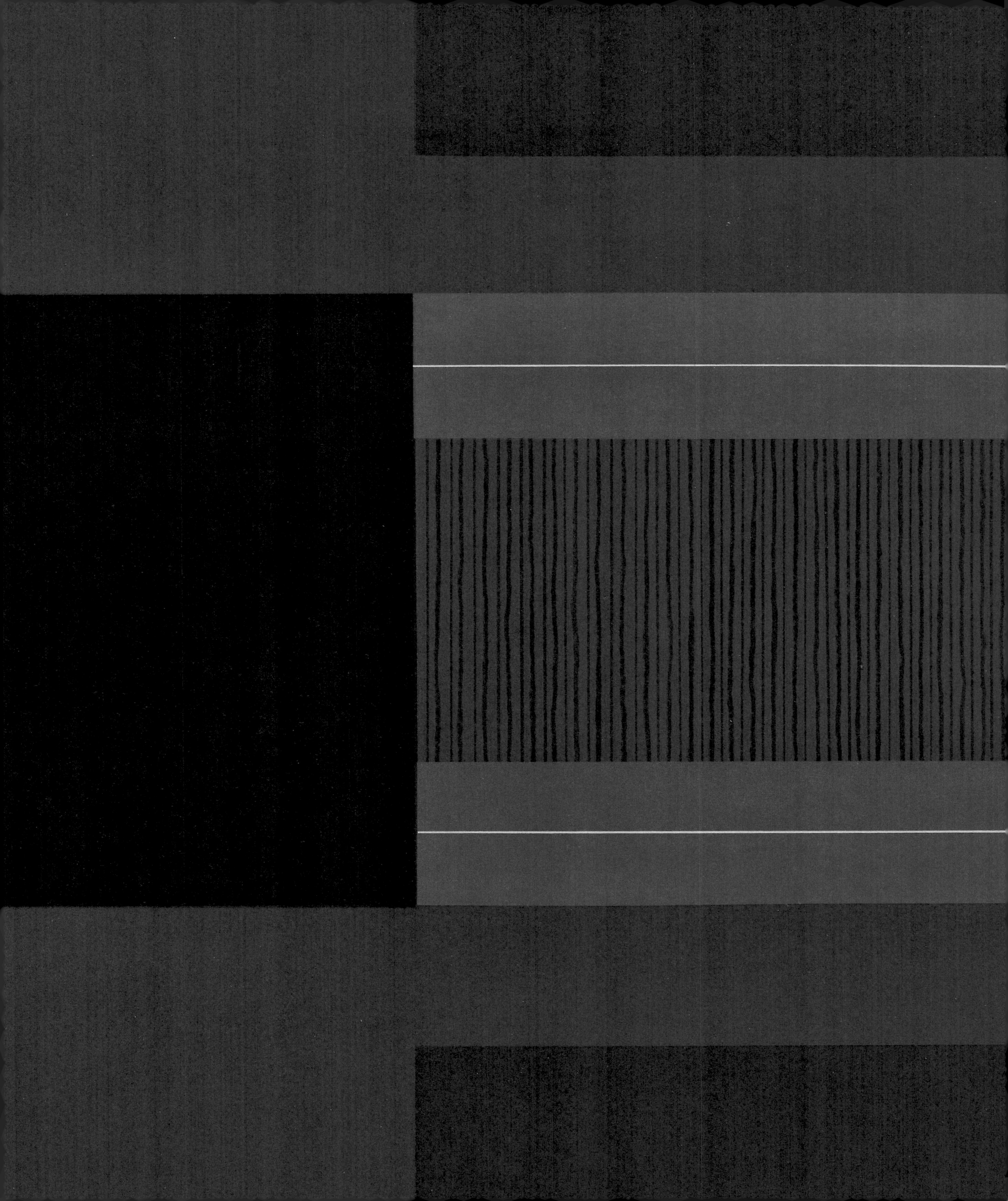

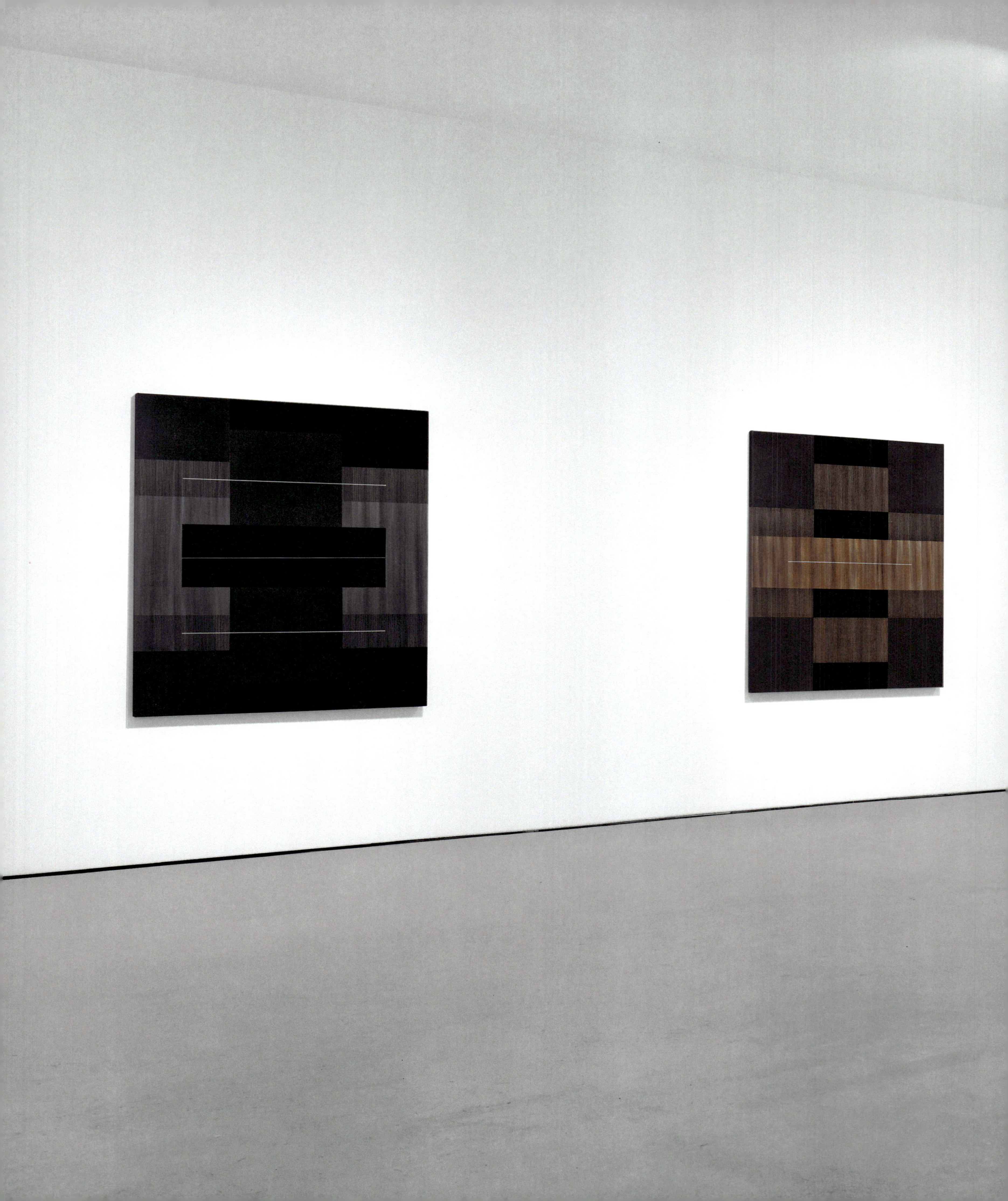

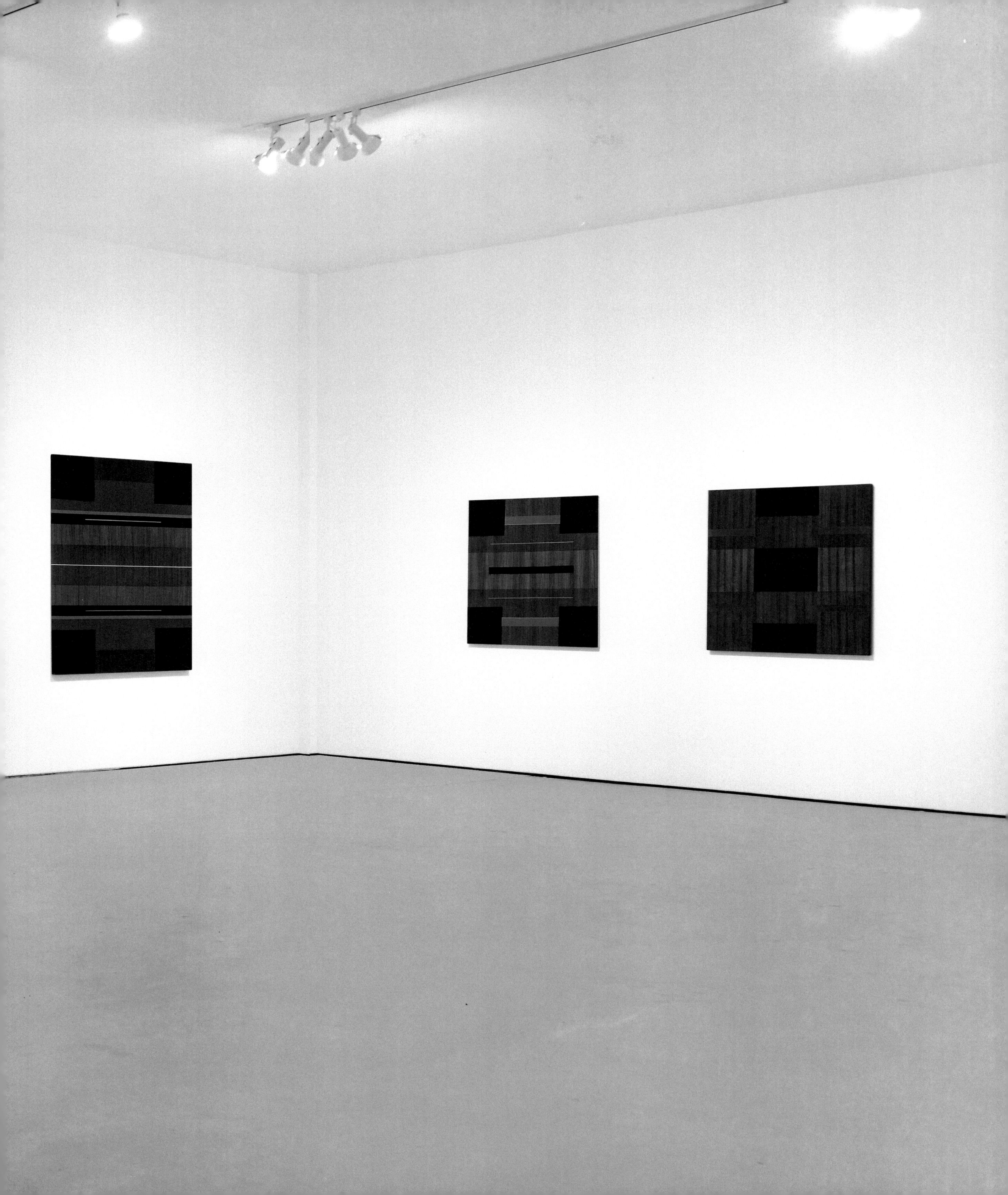

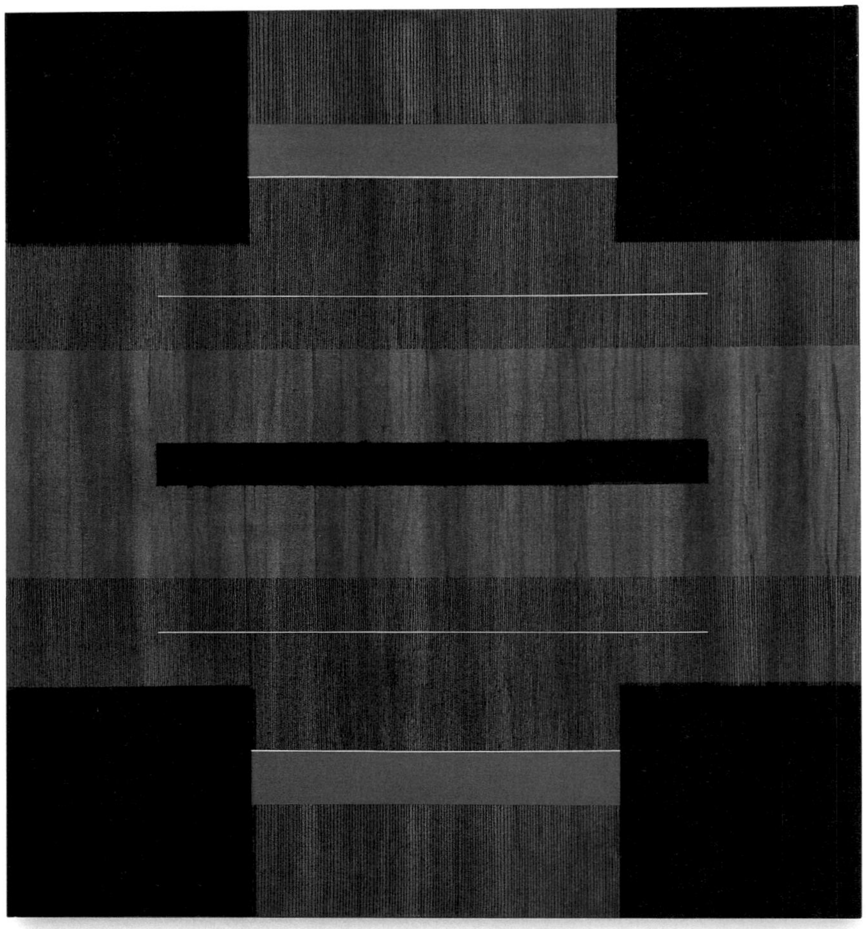

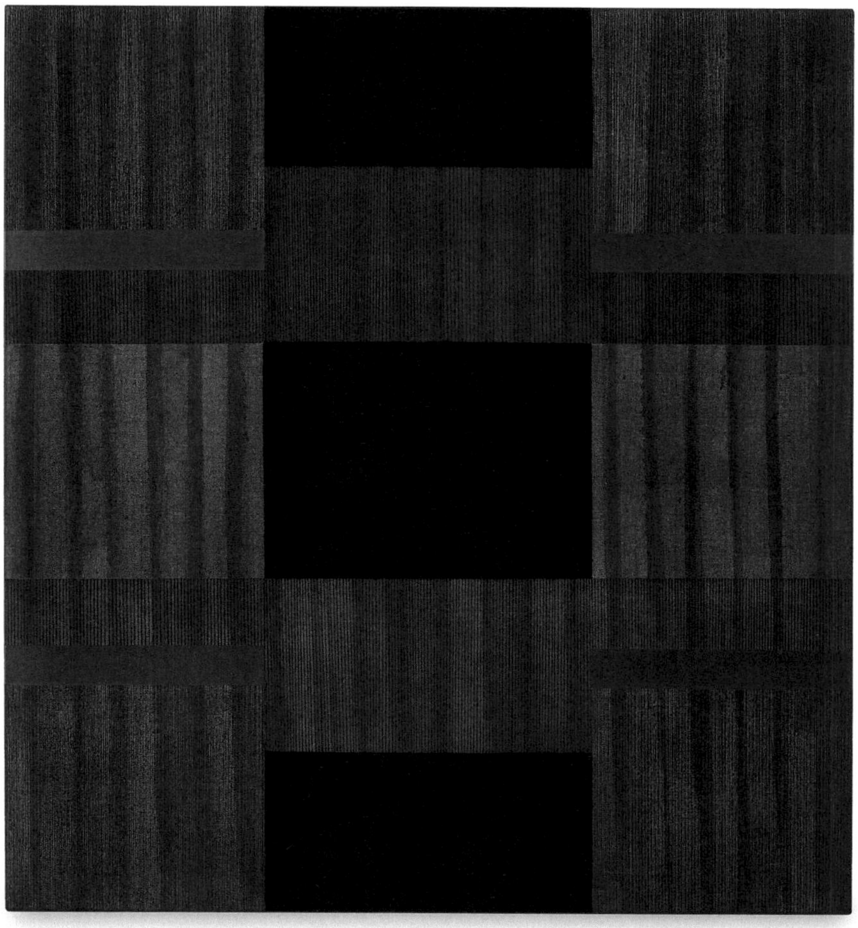

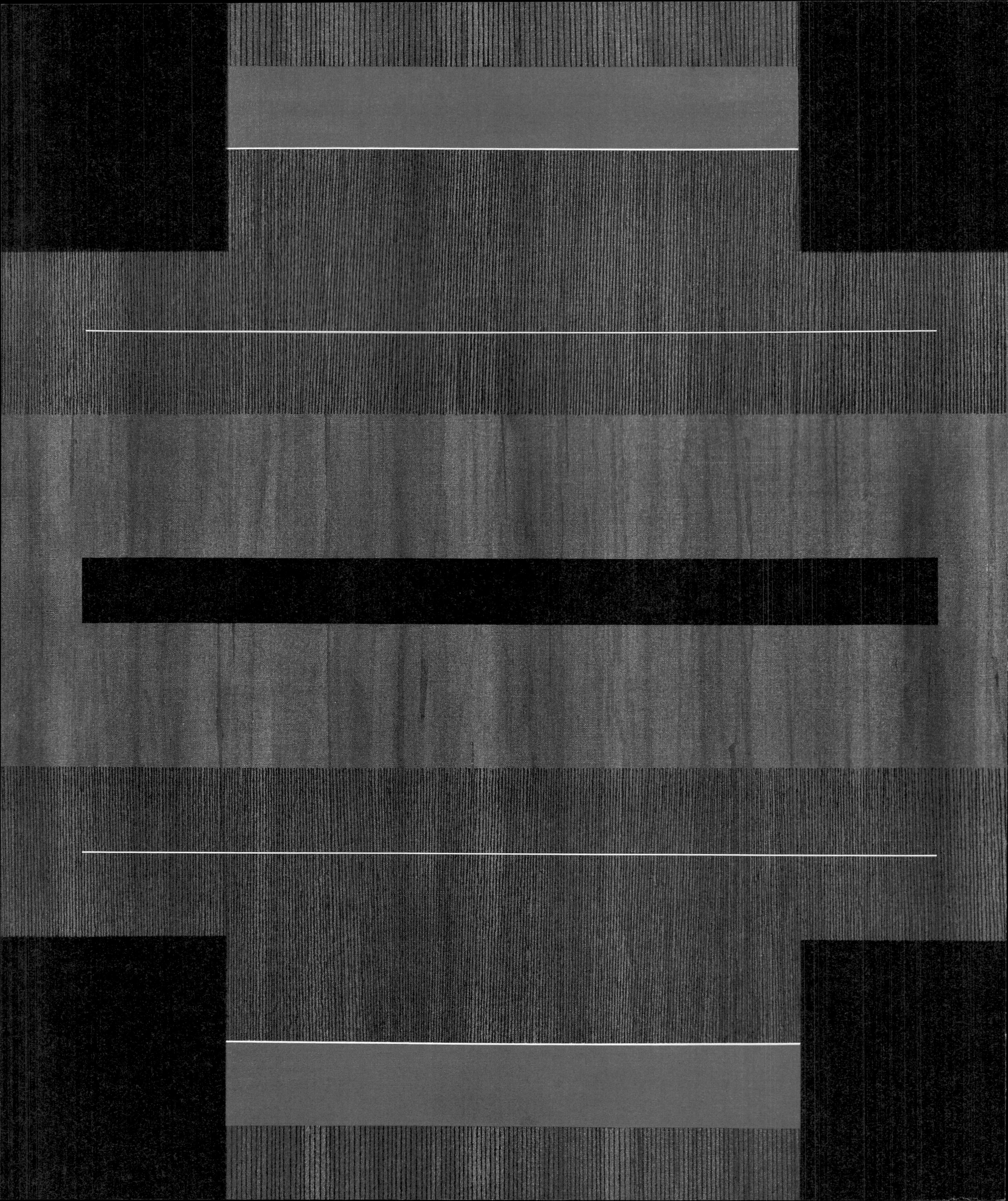

PREVIOUS SPREAD

PLATE 24 **IVORY/EBONY XVII**, 2022 acrylic on linen, 43 x 39 inches (109 x 99 cm) Collection of Mary Cardas and Lester Edelberg

PLATE 25 **IVORY/EBONY XVIII**, 2022 acrylic on linen, 43 x 39 inches (109 x 99 cm) Collection of Mary Cardas and Lester Edelberg

PLATE 26 **IVORY/EBONY XII**, 2022 acrylic on linen, 62 x 52 inches (157 x 132 cm) Tia Collection

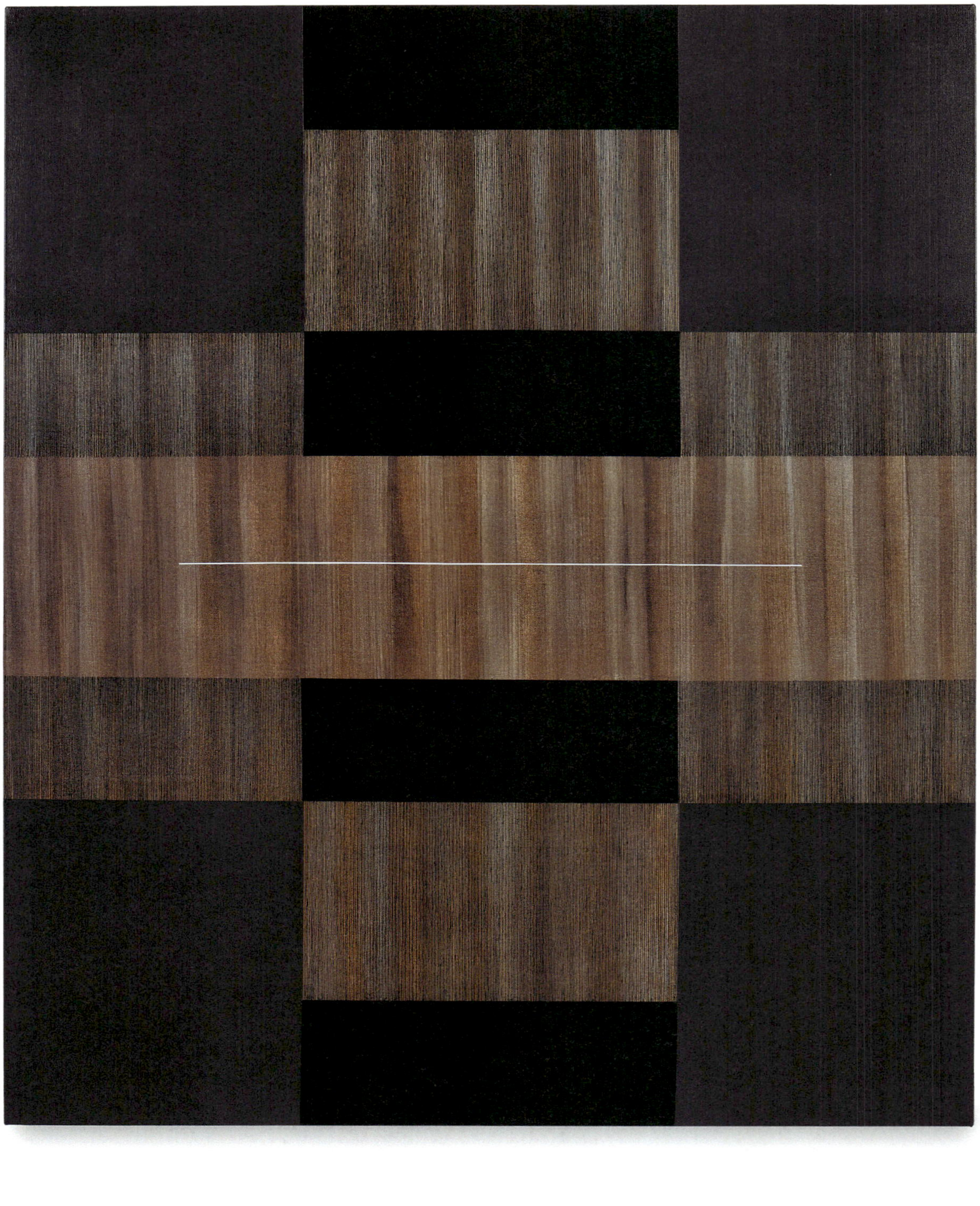

PLATE 27 **IVORY/EBONY XIV**, 2022 acrylic on linen, 62 x 52 inches (157 x 132 cm) Tia Collection

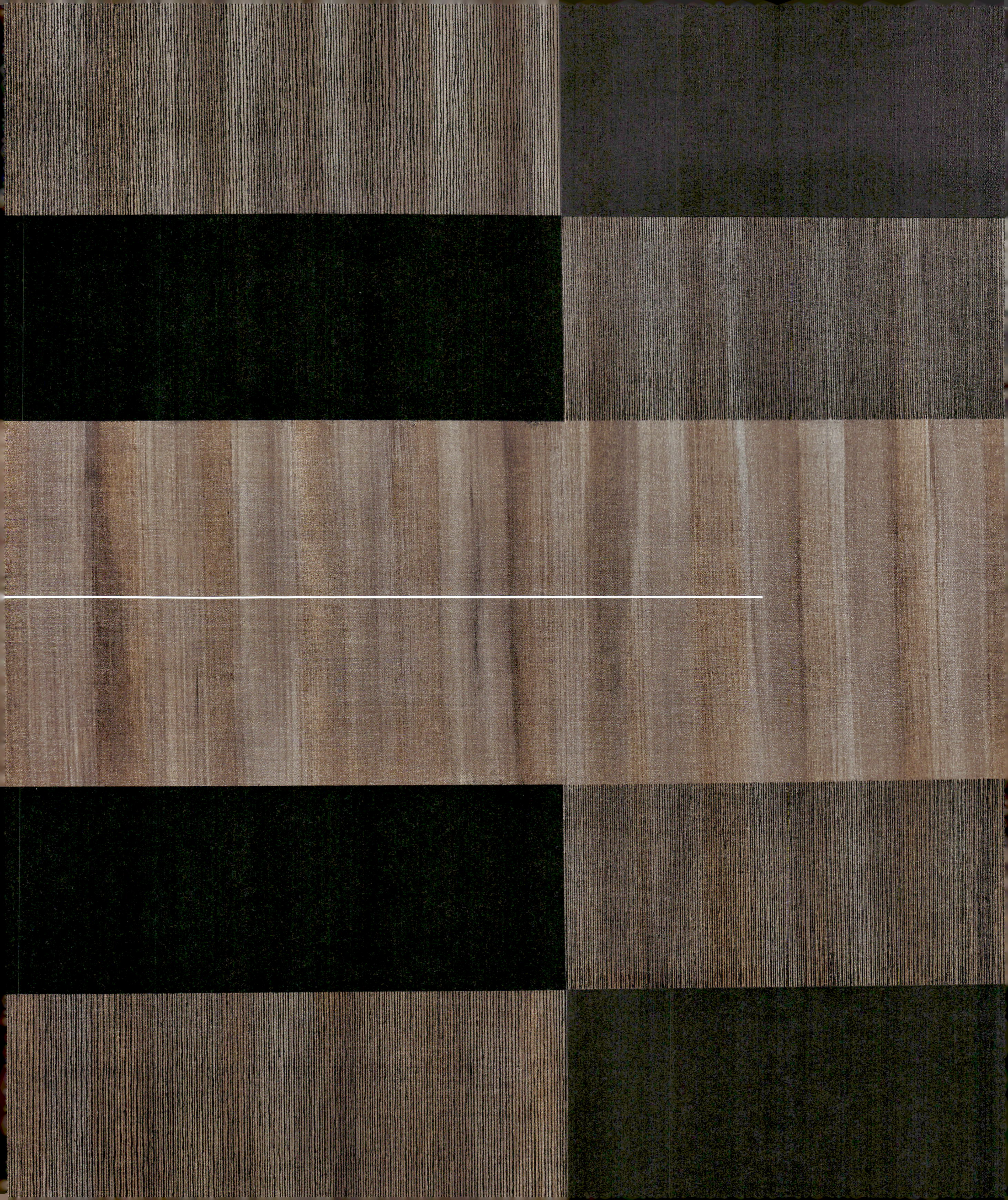

PLATE 28 **IVORY/EBONY XV**, 2022 acrylic on linen, 62 x 52 inches (157 x 132 cm) Tia Collection

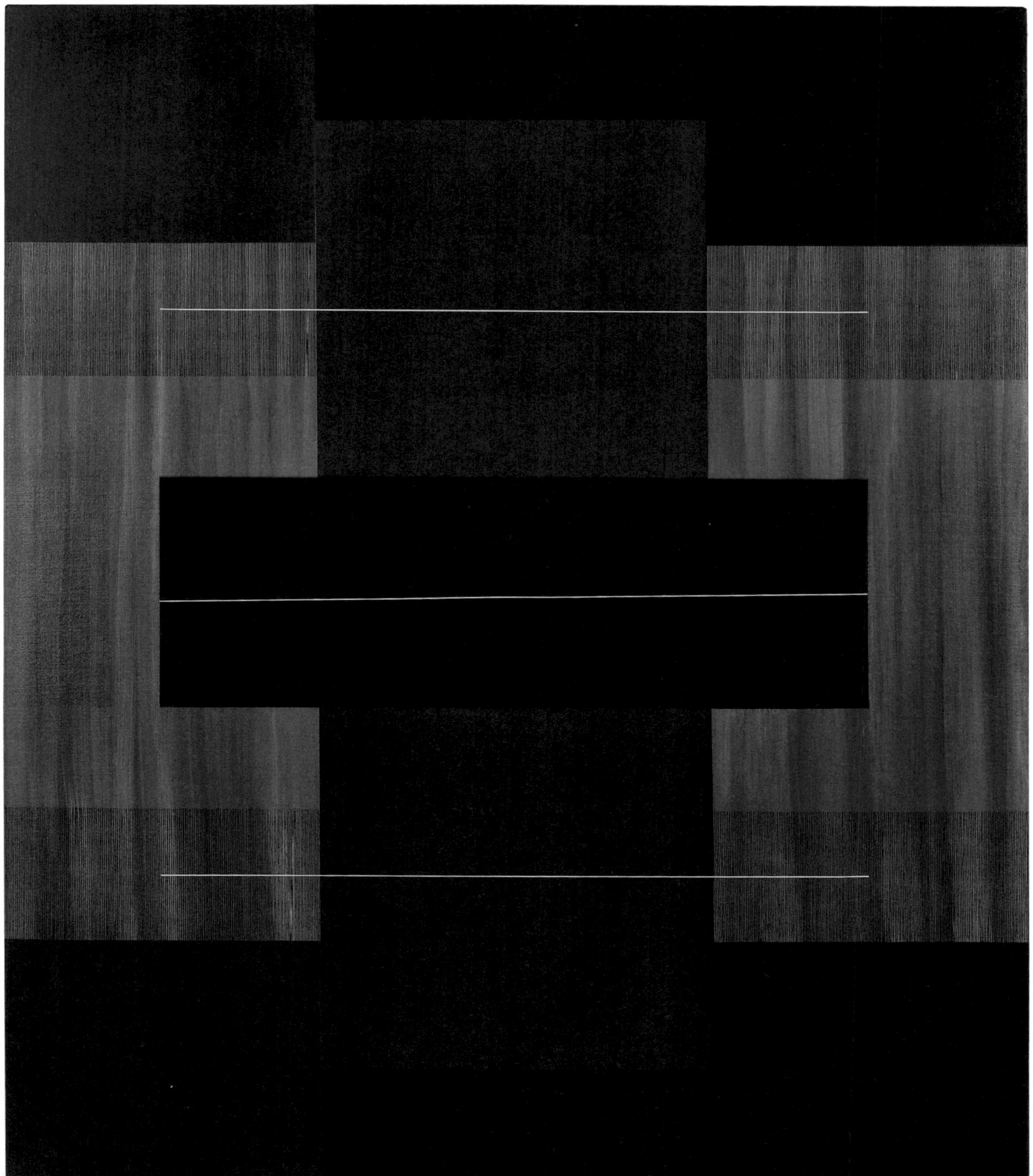

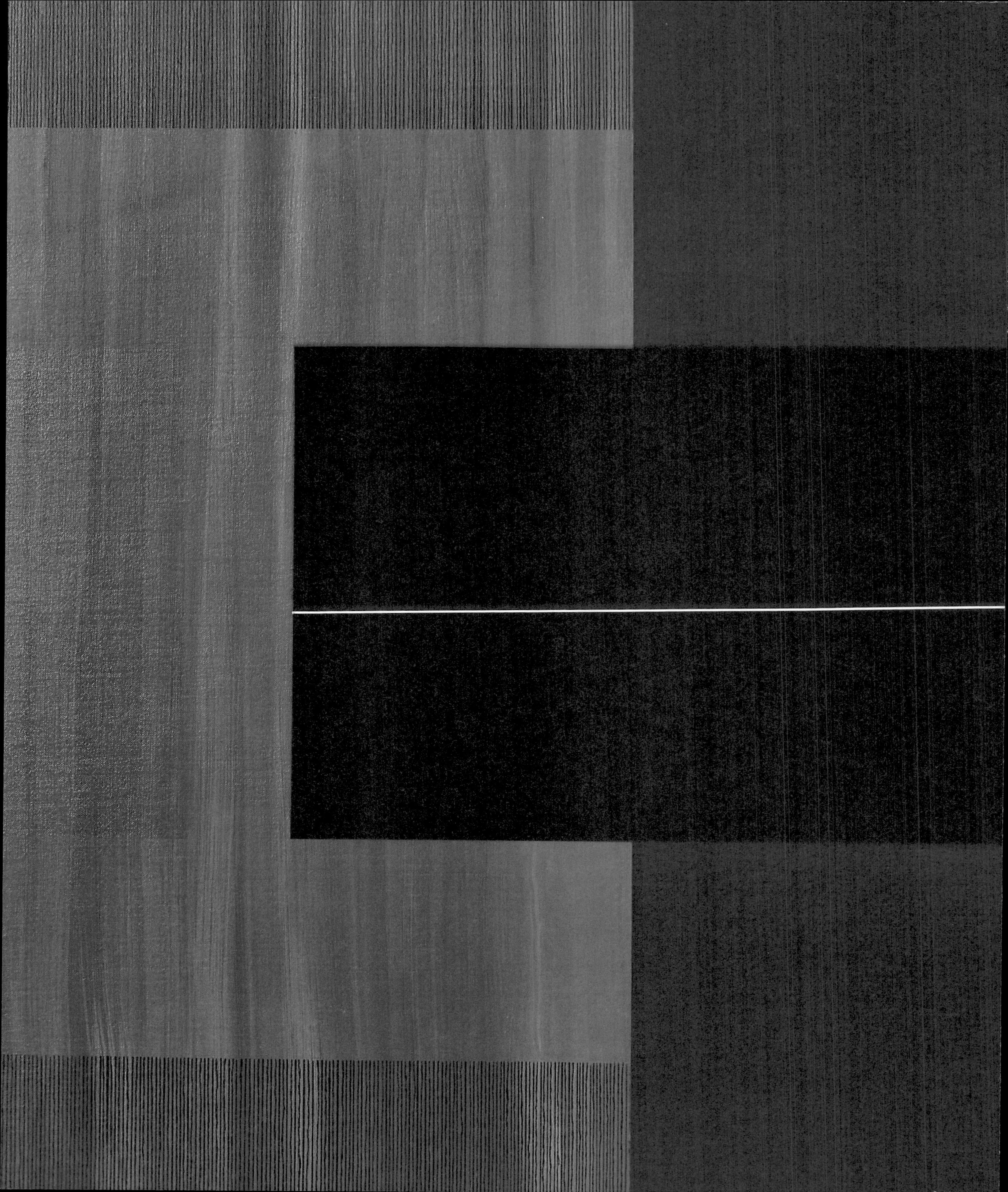

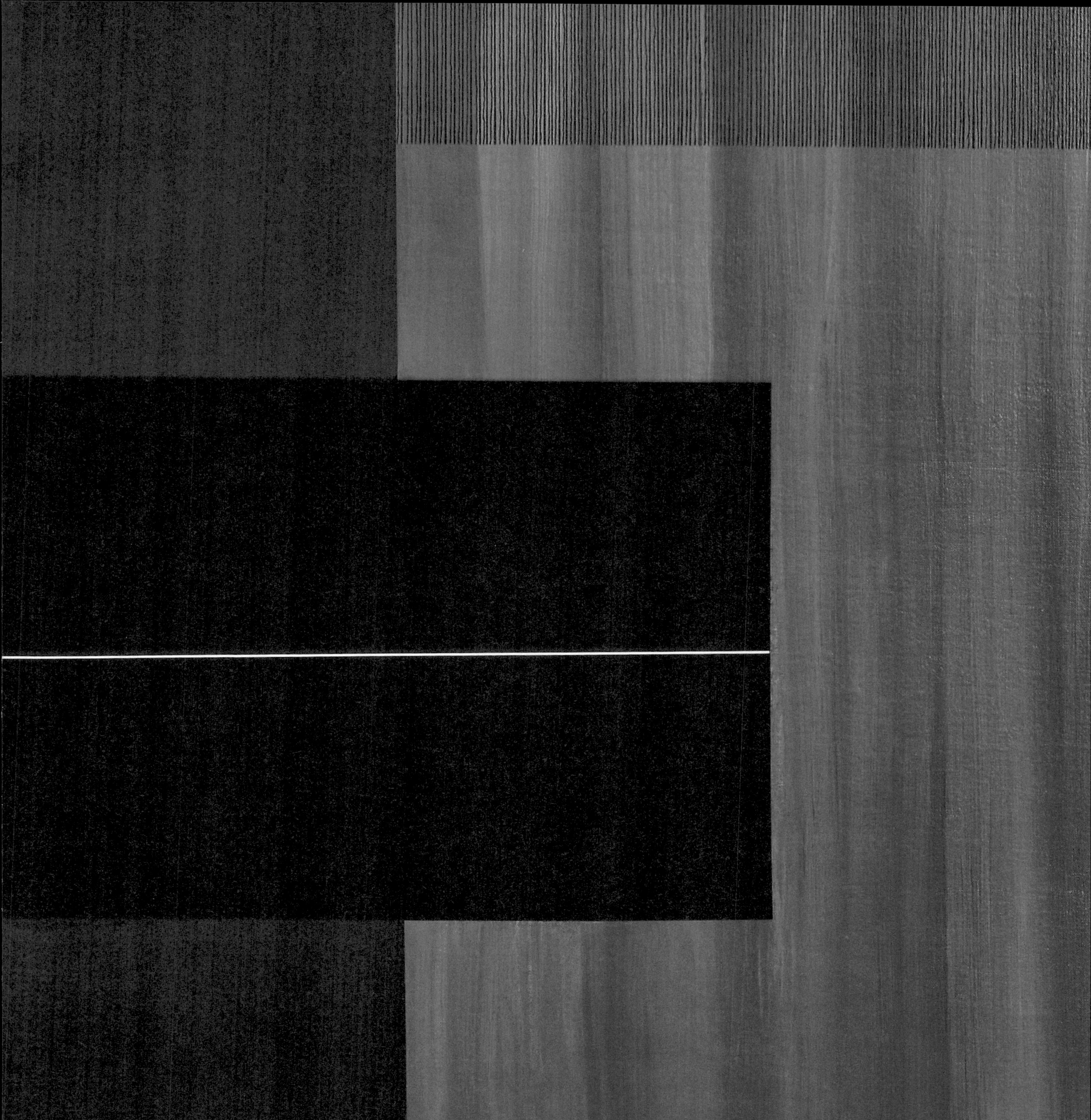

CONVERSATION

—MAX COLE WITH DAVID PAGEL

The following is a transcript of a conversation that took place on October 9, 2022 at SITE Santa Fe.

DAVID PAGEL:

Max, I want to start with your most recent works, by which I mean the ones from the last seven years, from the *Greek Crosses* to the *Ivory/Ebony* and *Ebony/Ivory* series.

To me, you're an extremely focused and concentrated artist and, for years, were refining and expanding what you were doing. And then, all of a sudden, *wham*, something big happened. Would you care to comment on that development?

MAX COLE:

First, I want to talk a bit about my relationship with you [David]. You started reviewing my work very early, when I first got out of graduate school and was very immature, but I had never met you until yesterday. I never have wanted to have an exchange of thoughts about my work because I value your depth of perception. I have appreciated that for many years, and I wanted that to stay pure, which it has.

It's rare that a critic sees work from over sixty years—it's actually been more than sixty years—with the only dialogue between the two of us being the work itself. That's pure, and you preserved that, so thank you.

My work has developed over the years. Every time it goes through a change, it alarms a lot of people because they don't understand that for something to grow, for it to stay alive, it has to change.

I have never wanted to endlessly repeat something just because it was successful at a certain point. I've seen that over time with many, many artists—you get to a certain point, have success, and you stay there. You die there. It becomes predictable the moment that you cease to take risks.

I'm not afraid of risk. I don't let anything leave the studio unless I'm completely convinced by it, so I must live with things for a while. Over time, it is possible to alter your perception; you can see things that aren't even there. It takes a little time for you to detach yourself enough from the work to really see it.

My work, by the way, is very slow in execution, but it is also very slow in communication. You don't instantly understand it; it has all kinds of nuances and subtleties that are extremely important.

One point that I want to make at the beginning of this conversation is how important this exhibition has been to me because a lot of the works here I have not seen since they were made. I make them, I box them up, put them in the storage, and go on to the next thing. Getting to come back to them much later is really wonderful because I get a fresh take on what I'm doing.

And along the way, I have made changes, but this exhibition shows me that those aren't really changes, they are just different points along the circle. The works I'm making in 2022 grew naturally from the ones I was making in the '70s, but you have to see an exhibition like this to fully realize that.

This is a really long answer to your question [*laughs*].

DP: No, I'm eager for more. So, the *Greek Crosses*—did they feel like something new? Like a circling back? Like an intensification? Was it a big moment when the first one happened?

MC: When I was in graduate school, I made the first *Greek Cross*—the one with the shirt on it [p. 40, center spread]—and I took a lot of criticism for it, which was valuable because it makes you think about what you're doing, if you believe in it or not.

And then I graduated. I got my MFA. You think you're a hot shot and you know everything there is to know when you don't actually know anything. I started showing early; I had two gallery shows, and then realized I don't know who I am. So, I shut myself in the studio. I was working in Pasadena in an old, condemned warehouse with electricity that came from a block away.

There wasn't any heat, and it was cold as ever. I caught my pants on fire backing up to a little wood stove, and after I beat the fire out, I decided I had to change. There was a gas line coming up in the alley but no meter, so I went to the junkyard and bought an old gas meter and installed it myself, running gas lines all over [*laughs*]. A plumber friend of mine came out and checked everything, and there weren't any leaks. I couldn't get a meter for the place because it was a condemned building, but I was warm there from then on.

In that space, I had no visitors, and I made no shows. I shut myself away until I finally understood my philosophy and my direction. I was making gigantic paintings that were about twelve feet high and maybe twenty feet wide. They split in the middle because I couldn't move them otherwise.

Somehow, someone from the Brand Art Center saw those works—they were in the studio; they hadn't gone out—and I ended up doing a show at the Brand. I no longer have those works. They were destroyed because it's hard to deal with a volume of works that massive. They were the absolute roots of what I'm doing now: repetitive elements and a collection of a lot of little marks. At that point, the marks were white; now they're black.

That's where the work came from.

I'm not a hustler; I've never gone out and tried to get anything for my work, an exhibition or anything else. I don't ask anybody to come to the studio. The work either lives by itself or it doesn't, so I'm not interested in helping it along. All the things that come artificially can't be trusted. Things that come of their own volition, you'd better pay attention to because there's a reason for them to come, and that gives them validity.

DP: I'm glad you brought up that piece, Max. I think it was the only piece in your show that would be called a work of found-object art, with the fabric clothing put right on it. When I went through the show, there was a powerful resonance between that one and the *Greek Crosses*. Then when I went back—I never read titles until after I look at the work—and read the title; I think it's called *Crucifixion*.

MC: It is called *Crucifixion*.

DP: That has, on one hand, explicit religious references, but for me, it's more than that. It's also about a kind of suffering and sacrifice, and I thought that those things might be important to you in your work—

MC: Well, those are valid comments. As I mentioned, I took tremendous criticism for that painting.

DP: Because?

MC: Well, people thought that it was sacrilegious, and they also thought that that was blood on the shirttail, when it's actually paint. I just took off the shirt and put it on the canvas.

DP: Well, it is sacrilegious [*laughs*].

MC: [*Laughs*] It was important to me what happened there. There were many letters to the editor in the Tucson newspaper protesting that work, that children shouldn't be exposed to it and so on. They wouldn't let me respond for a long time, but finally they published a little article I wrote.

A month later, Tucson made me "Citizen of the Month."

I was amazed that art could arouse such passion. I think for it to do that, the work has to be completely honest—I don't think it can be faked. That painting has been important to the rest of my development—it defines the horizontal/vertical as a basic format, and that's all I need. I'm not trying to reproduce a mood or anything like that.

Obviously, there's an intensity to making the work; you can't make all those millions of little lines without thinking about every single one of them. They have to be perfect—you can't change them. You put them down once, and that's it. It's not labor. It becomes a process very akin to meditation, and it has a purity. I'm not talking in terms of religion; I'm talking in terms of the human spirit.

So, the works evolved, getting more and more horizontal. By the way, that one very large horizontal painting was done at a time in New York when I thought: "I'll never show another painting again in my life." It was the era of Julian Schnabel bad painting.

DP: Tastes had changed.

MC: I had been mistakenly identified as a Constructivist. I am not. Constructivism often implies a total involvement in intellectual composition and content. I'm the other part of the Russian Constructivist movement, the Malevich part, the part that dealt with the spiritual. They are two separate things.

Russian Constructivism via Malevich did not mean sentimentality. That's a very superficial interpretation. I do believe in the spirit, and so the intellectual alone is not enough to me. That's why I'm there.

DP: For me, when I saw the *Greek Crosses*, I didn't think of a historical crucifixion or anything in the past. I looked at those as a person, which is a body, standing there saying: "Here I am. This is it. This is everything." For me, the *Greek Crosses* intensify what had been happening in your work up until that moment. It really felt like a being or a presence was in that room with me. Does that resonate with any of your thoughts?

MC: Well, I haven't thought about it in that way, but I think that probably is a part of it. I see it as an opposition of two forces, and that establishes an equilibrium, particularly when it's on a square format. The new works are the first vertical ones I've made since I was a kid. They come closer to the traditional cross that you're alluding to; working with the cross form is loaded with connotations.

I'm not dealing with it from a traditional religious perspective, which differs from a spiritual perspective. The spiritual has always been a big consideration for me throughout my work. I'm not Catholic. I've been invited to the Vatican three times, and I've also made a lot of exhibitions in cathedrals in Europe. I was very impressed with Pope Benedict. He didn't care if I was Catholic or not. We speak a common language that's above all that stuff.

To me, it's essential that art be a spiritual communication, and it only works if the communication goes two ways; otherwise, you're just throwing stuff out there. I'm not interested in that. I'm gratified and I'm validated by the fact that people can understand where this work is coming from.

I don't care if it's intellectual, but if there's a connection on a spiritual level, that's what this is about, as I don't think art is meant to provide any answers. It's just another language that people can communicate with, and I think that it can be very uplifting.

DP: Yes. I'd like to circle back and pick up on the idea of isolation. Isolation was important to you in your studio in Pasadena—you had done a couple shows and then decided: "I've got to figure out what's going on for me before this public conversation." And you didn't show for about five years when you hunkered down in your studio?

MC: I quit. I quit entirely.

DP: And that was essential for your development?

MC: It absolutely was.

DP: I want to link that back to something you said about your childhood in another interview you did with Douglas Dreishpoon. You said something like: "Well, this isolation from art growing up was really good for me because I never had to unlearn any bad work. Heck, we didn't even have Sunday painters."

MC: That's true. Well, I have to tell you something about my childhood first. I remember the day World War II broke out. My father came home from work and said that Pearl Harbor had been bombed and we had to move. We were right up the road in Mancos, Colorado. I remember that day clearly, and I was only three years old.

So, we moved back to Kansas, where most of the family was, and then he got work as a heavy-equipment mechanic, big earth-moving machines and all that kind of stuff. They were building airstrips all over the Southwest. A lot of counties had military airstrips, and my father worked on a lot of those, as well as on huge dam projects.

Because of that, we moved all the time; by the time I was in the sixth grade, I had gone to sixteen different schools. There was zero continuity, so I established my own continuity: I made art from the time I was a little kid on. I established a continuing world because it was portable, and I got acceptance in the new schools because I could make art really well. It was a portable identity for me, not for anybody else. There's never been a time that I didn't make art for very private reasons. I had to establish some kind of thread that connected everything together, so that's what I did, and I could do it anywhere.

DP: Along with isolation, I also wanted to talk to you about identity. Identity is a big deal right now, and I wanted to ask you about your identity as an artist, but you kind of answered that question already. It seems to me, without putting words in your mouth, that you established a place and a continuum for yourself as a human being through art. Your art was an essential element of your identity from when you were three years old.

MC: I would add that there is no wall between my self and my art—they are one and the same. They are melded. Art is not something that I can put to the side, and it's always been that way. It's never going to change because I have actually lived art. It's become who I am.

And the isolation factor is really important. I don't have very much respect or need for raw emotion. It's superficial and is connected to the ego, and it's very wasteful. Doesn't mean I don't get ticked off occasionally because I do—

DP: I wish you could tell that to a few of my friends.

MC: [*Laughs*]—but that's not what my life is.

DP: Right.

MC: And it is a totally individual thing. It does not have to be connected to religion or any other thing. Recognition that the spirit exists is a recognition of a greater reality.

There is a connection between what I'm doing and things like physics. There's truth in physics. The definition of a line is a moving point in space, and the energy of making that line remains embedded in the line. That's why I'm using one. There is a connection between spirituality and physics, and I think the more we find out about the universe, the more exciting it's going to get because it's going to expand a whole lot of things.

DP: Did you know when you were young that art was essential to your life, or did that realization come later? Was it a slow dawning or a bolt of lightning?

MC: It's always been essential to my life. I'm going to tell you an embarrassing story that I haven't told anybody. When I was three, I found a yellow crayon —I didn't have any pockets, and so I carried it in my nostril [*laughs*]. I'd take it out and draw, and, eventually, when it got really small, it got lodged way up in my nose. They took me to the doctor, and they couldn't get it out, so my father took me outside and gave me one hell of a spanking. I squealed so hard that the crayon flew out.

DP: [*Laughs*] Do you still have the drawings? Do you still have the crayon?

MC: No, it was a tiny little thing. It was just enough to clog up my breathing. I have always drawn. When I was in the first grade, I got in horrible trouble because I found a piece of chalk—I could't read then—and I picked it up and drew the F-word all over the whole school. I had no idea what it meant.

DP: [*Laughs*] That was your conceptual piece?

MC: I was sent to the principal, and I didn't know what I did. He finally let me go back to class because he could tell I didn't know what it was.

DP: Did you ever think making art would be a career, or was that—?

MC: No, I never thought about it as a career. When I was very young, I got married, and my husband died in a car wreck when I was twenty.

So okay, I've got to do something. We didn't have any money. I've got to go to school. My first semester, I went to junior college, and I took drawing classes. Then I transferred to a university and took art classes because I've always been an artist. While I was there—I think I told you this story—about the black paintings?

DP: No.

MC: Well, I started making all-black paintings. Good students got a little studio, and so I had a studio even though I was an undergrad. There was a little gallery there. It was on a Sunday, and the gallery was between shows—they've got all these nice blank walls. I wanted to see what those black paintings looked like hanging up on nice clean white walls.

DP: Naturally.

MC: So, I hung them, and somebody from the psychology department happened by and saw these black paintings. On Monday morning, I got a call from the department chairman saying that I had to go see the psychology people because of those black paintings. What's wrong with black? If you look at the universe, it's mostly black. Black has mystery. Doesn't mean I've got problems. I decided that the psychology department actually has a lot of problems. They're afraid of the dark, and I'm not going to go and see them because I'm just fine. So, I didn't. Not long after, Malevich was shown for the first time, and you could even see a reproduction in this country. That's an affirmation, and that is the start of this direction that I've pursued all these years.

I have to say it has been incredibly rich and rewarding. It is so grand for an artist to be able to communicate with another person based on what's in your soul, and the art does that. It can happen.

DP: Yeah, it's good stuff. In an earlier interview, when you were asked about the value of experience, and if working now was a lot different from working when you had just started out, you answered: "No. I'm still trying to discover stuff in my work. Anybody who thinks that they know the answers is either a bore or a fool."

MC: That's true. I can think of nothing more useless than marching in place. The mysteries can't be solved. They're immense. They're beyond the comprehension of any one person. This quest is about those mysteries, and I find it a necessary part of pushing forward, which I intend to do until the day I die, even if I'm making things like a postcard. Size doesn't have anything to do with it. At a certain age, you have to prove your toughness and your prowess and all that stuff.

DP: The big paintings.

MC: Well, I don't need to prove that, so I'm perfectly comfortable working with whatever I can. The most gratifying thing that I can think of being an old artist who's been around this long is the fact that I'm communicating to every single one of you [the audience members] or you wouldn't be here. If that can't happen, then you're talking to yourself. It's much more gratifying to be talking to someone.

DP: I'd like to go back to what you said about physics and a line being the movement between two points. I've heard you say that what you're after in your paintings, what you're trying to capture, is the quivering energy of the mark-making. Could you say a little bit more about that?

MC: It's keeping that consistency. It's never perfect, and it quivers because I don't measure anything. Measuring is boring; it's mechanical. You're never able to complete a line without being interrupted—you've got to sleep, and eat, and answer the phone, but you have to get your head in that place. The fact that it's not possible to get your head exactly in that place, that's where the quiver comes from. The energy moving that dot to create the line becomes part of the painting.

DP: You've also talked about intuition in your work, which I think is important to bring up. I think you said something like, "I never know what the painting is going to look like when I begin. I just get started, and it comes out how it has to be."

MC: That's true. I can't plan my paintings. I can set the format and scale, but I don't know what's going to happen on a painting until I get in it. I just start. It develops a certain characteristic, a certain mood, a certain amount of intensity, and I just get on that same thread and carry it through.

There are times when I can't do that; they're failed paintings, which I destroy because I don't try to patch anything up and make it something it's not. It's either a complete statement or it gets destroyed. I don't worry about communication because of all of you here [in the audience]. It is so gratifying to have this communication because it means I haven't been talking to myself for sixty years.

DP: Yes. I also wanted to talk to you about a couple of F-words: "failure" and "fear." You just brought up the idea of failure—when you're working on something that isn't right and it gets chucked—

MC: Yeah. Well, if it fails, it does not have life, and there's no reason for it to exist. It keeps you humble if you fail once in a while. You get knocked off your ego real fast. I can think of nothing more boring than hitting a hole-in-one every time you hit the golf ball.

DP: —or thinking you did.

MC: Yeah [*laughs*].

DP: That's even worse. When it's a failure, do you recognize that early in the process or really late? Or is it always different?

MC: Midway. You can tell things are being forced, and the reason is usually you can't get focused. Well, if you can't get focused, you shouldn't be working, so those paintings have no reason to exist.

I think Jackson Pollock probably had the same feeling—that a painting was forced—every once in a while. I never knew Pollock, but he was totally engaged in his work, as am I. I would imagine, working emotionally as he did, there must have been times when the same block happened. He worked with emotion, which I love. I do not condemn emotion; it's just not my direction.

DP: You're after a kind of unforcedness over things—

MC: Yes, yes.

DP: —where you follow what's happening, and it feels... what? Graceful?

MC: Yes, it feels like a sense of completion, a sense of calmness. I can't say satisfaction—

DP: No, that's too personal.

MC: —because if you reach satisfaction, you're going to stop painting. A sense of completing a step, I would say, but it has to be open-ended. I have no idea where the works are going to go. I really don't. I know they won't exist if they aren't good. I'll destroy them. I don't expect there to be any major changes because I'm not about to change my personality—not at this point—so, it's going to be things that grow out.

Life is pretty much a circle, which I realized when we put this show up, because I was afraid these new paintings were not going to be related to what I'd done before. They are directly related. The circle is far from closed—from the new paintings that are in this exhibition to when I finally stop making art, when I'm either blind or dead—there's a gap there because I'm not finished with this, by any means. They're never going to be gigantic again because I will continue to refuse a studio assistant. So, they may get awfully small before I'm finished.

DP: Yeah, that sense of unforcedness or that calmness, to me, really comes through in the two primarily white or lighter-colored, horizontal pieces hanging next to each other in the second-to-last gallery [plates 14 and 15]. You stand before one and think: "Yes. Everything is in its right place, and it's just perfect." And then you stand before the next one and think: "This is really different, and it's also perfect." To me, that's a really lovely moment. It's not perfect in that it feels closed, but everything just feels right, like when the waves are lapping on the shore. Just the rhythm.

MC: I am so grateful for this exhibition because those two paintings that you're talking about, I made them a long time ago, and I boxed them up. I hadn't seen them until they were hanging on the wall in here.

DP: They're good ones.

MC: I love them. I hadn't seen them for maybe thirty years.

DP: Each one has its own rhythm, its own hum, its own pace, and its own atmosphere. From far away, you might think they look almost the same, but they're not even close to the same—

MC: Well, they changed a lot over time, as, I think, your body changes, the way you see things changes, your experiences, and where you are. All those things are bound to have an effect.

I was wondering where, in this spectrum of my work, are these new paintings? For me, it's an affirmation that they're a part of this progression; that question has been solved for me for this exhibition. I really appreciate it, and it was important to have that last room be just current work.

DP: Do you want to talk a little bit about tantric art?

MC: Well, you can ask the question.

DP: [*Laughs*] It seems to me it's an interest you've had, not in terms of how the work looks but in terms of the way the work functions. Is that true?

MC: Well, yes. As you can see, I don't pay any attention at all to composition, as I don't think all those traditional things necessarily apply to everything. You can make your own rules.

You have things built into your sensibility that you've been conditioned about for years: composition and all that stuff. You don't even have to think about that. That's stuff that's ingrained, so I think I rely on instinct. I'm not sure I'm answering your question.

DP: What I was thinking about with tantric work was the egolessness, that it wasn't about the artist. It was about doing something in the world—there was a quest for some kind of harmony—which I think puts you in the same universe—

MC: Well, yeah, I try to keep ego out of it. It's the "Big I," and I think the "Big I" must be set aside because you can't get past it. The ego is so tied to emotion that it doesn't allow a connection to the spirit. Not to invalidate every other artist who has worked with ego, but it's not what I'm concerned with. I'm concerned with going beyond the sense of self.

Everybody has emotion, including me, but I don't want it in my art, so I shut it out. In a sense, it's stepping beyond a certain sense of self. I have an ego. Everybody does. But I don't think it has to be a part of art. For me, it's completely nonessential because it becomes a barrier to the spiritual.

DP: Yeah, and the art is about getting beyond the self to something else?

MC: Yes. I think every culture has had aspects of what we're speaking of. It may look different formally, but every culture has approached spirituality not by emotion but by something else.

ACKNOWLEDGMENTS

It is a rare opportunity for an artist to see so much of the breadth and depth of their own work in a single exhibition. It is with deep gratitude that I wish to sincerely acknowledge and thank the many people who made possible the 2022/2023 exhibition, *Endless Journey*. This thoughtful presentation of work, spanning over sixty years, could not have been done without the skill, hard work, and artistic understanding of the entire staff at SITE Santa Fe. I express my special appreciation to Louis Grachos for his strong and tireless support over the years, as well as to Brandee Caoba for her keen sense of design and curatorial skill. The Board of Directors of SITE Santa Fe has been incredibly generous throughout this project, and I wholeheartedly thank these dedicated people.

I especially wish to extend my gratitude to David Pagel for his decades of meaningful reviews and insight into my work, and, of course, for traveling to SITE Santa Fe to finally meet in person for our *My Life in Art* discussion. Thank you to Charlotte Jackson for her support, not only as a gallerist but as a friend.

Though I cannot name you all here, I appreciate the countless others who have understood and championed my work over the years, and the numerous new connections made because of this exhibition.

—MAX COLE

CONTRIBUTORS

MAX COLE was born in Kansas in 1937, and she grew up in the Southwest. She earned her bachelor's degree in 1961 from Fort Hays University in Kansas, and three years later, she earned her master's degree from the University of Arizona in Tucson. Since then, she has lived in Los Angeles, New York, and Europe. She now resides and works in northern New Mexico.

Cole has received honors and fellowships from the University of Arizona, the National Endowment for the Arts, the Pollack / Krasner Foundation, the Adolph Gottlieb Foundation, The Roswell Museum and Art Center, and The Joseph and Anni Albers Foundation. She attended a Contemporary Artist's Meeting with Pope Benedict XVI at the Sistine Chapel in 2009.

Cole's career commenced in 1976 with a four-person exhibition entitled *New Abstract Painting* at the Los Angeles County Museum of Art. Between 1979 and 1984, her work was featured in four exhibitions at the Sidney Janis Gallery in New York City. She was a part of two exhibitions at Albright Knox, one in 1979 and the next in 2007. In 2004, she held a solo exhibition at the Kolumba Museum in Cologne, Germany. Her work was permanently installed in Italy's Panza Collection in 2000, and she was one of two US artists included in *The Splendor of Truth, the Beauty of Charity* in the Vatican in 2011. She had a solo exhibition in 2012 at the Mies van der Rohe Haus in Berlin entitled *To the Line*. In 2013, her solo exhibition, *Meditations*, was held at St. Peter's Cathedral in Cologne. Her work was also featured in *Guiseppe Panza di Biumo: American Dialogs, Ca' Pesare* in 2015, for which the International Gallery of Contemporary Art in Venice collaborated with The Museum of Contemporary Art in Los Angeles, The Guggenheim in New York, and the Panza Collection in Italy. Cole's paintings were most recently acquired by the Tia Collection in Santa Fe, New Mexico. She has exhibited work in numerous other museums in Europe and the United States, including her 2022 survey exhibition at SITE Santa Fe, and her work continues in an endless journey.

DAVID PAGEL is an art critic, curator, and professor of art theory and history at Claremont Graduate University in Claremont, California. His reviews and essays have appeared in the *Los Angeles Times*, *Brooklyn Rail*, and *Artforum*. Recent publications include *Jim Shaw* (Lund Humphries, 2019) and *Talking Beauty: A Conversation Between Joseph Raffael and David Pagel about Art, Love, Death, and Creativity* (Zero+, 2018), as well as catalog essays on Jay DeFeo, Augustine Kofie, Brenda Goodman, Gajin Fujita, and Dion Johnson. Recently organized exhibitions include *re:Socializing—art out of quarantine* and *Kenneth Noland/Auguste Rodin/Ian Trout*, both at Claremont Graduate University. A self-taught diorama builder and an avid cyclist, Pagel is a seven-time winner of the California Triple Crown.

Operating on the belief that the arts—all arts—are vital to our culture, RADIUS BOOKS is a 501(c)(3) non-profit organization with a focus on photography and fine art book publishing. In addition to publishing, RADIUS BOOKS encourages aspiring artists through educational workshops and community events and distributes books of artistic and educational value for a wide audience.

RADIUS BOOKS donates copies of every title we publish into a nationwide network of libraries and schools, with the hope and expectation that these books will reach and inspire new audiences.

Support for *Endless Journey* is generously provided by:

SITE Santa Fe Board of Directors

SITE Santa Fe Annual Exhibition Fund

Charlotte Jackson Fine Art

Anonymous

Art Santa Fe Presents, Inc.

Mary Cardas and Les Edelberg

Carolyn Eason and James Rubin

Dalia and Michael Engler

Jayne and Michael Flinn

Pat Hall

Nancy Parker Magoon

Joan and Mitchell Markow

Linda and William McQuillan

Henry R. Muñoz III

Christophe A. Olson - Roebling Endowment & Josed Granados

Melba and Ted Whatley

Rosina Yue

RADIUS BOOKS
227 E. Palace Ave., Suite W, Santa Fe, NM 87501
t: (505) 983-4068 radiusbooks.org

Available through
D.A.P. / DISTRIBUTED ART PUBLISHERS
75 Broad Street, Suite 630, New York, NY 10004
t: (212) 627-1999 artbook.com

ISBN 978-1-955161-32-9

Library of Congress Cataloging-in-Publication Data
available from the publisher upon request.

DESIGN: David Chickey & Mat Patalano
EDITING: Nick Larsen
PHOTOGRAPHY: Brad Trone
PRE-PRESS + PRINTING: Editoriale Bortolazzi-Stei, Verona, Italy